DROP SHIPPING AS A MARKETING FUNCTION

Recent Titles from Quorum Books

Expert Systems in Finance and Accounting
Robert J. Thierauf

The Law and Occupational Injury, Disease, and Death
Warren Freedman

Judgment in International Accounting: A Theory of Cognition, Cultures, Language, and Contracts
Ahmed Belkaoui

The Evolution of Foreign Banking Institutions in the United States: Developments in International Finance
Faramarz Damanpour

Corporate Planning, Human Behavior, and Computer Simulation: Forecasting Business Cycles
Roy L. Nersesian

The Valuation and Investment Merits of Diamonds
Sarkis J. Khoury

Market-Oriented Pricing: Strategies for Management
Michael H. Morris and Gene Morris

The Divestiture Option: A Guide for Financial and Corporate Planning Executives
Richard J. Schmidt

International Perspectives on Trade Promotion and Assistance
S. Tamer Cavusgil and Michael R. Czinkota, editors

The Promise of American Industry: An Alternative Assessment of Problems and Prospects
Donald L. Losman and Shu-jan Liang

Global Corporate Intelligence: Opportunities, Technologies, and Threats in the 1990s
George S. Roukis, Hugh Conway, and Bruce Charnov, editors

The Process of Change in American Banking: Political Economy and the Public Purpose
Jeremy F. Taylor

DROP SHIPPING
AS A MARKETING
FUNCTION

A Handbook
of Methods
and
Policies

Nicholas T. Scheel

QUORUM BOOKS
New York • Westport, Connecticut • London

Library of Congress Cataloging-in-Publication Data

Scheel, Nicholas T.
    Drop shipping as a marketing function : a handbook of methods and
policies / Nicholas T. Scheel.
       p. cm.
    Includes bibliographical references.
    ISBN 0-89930-532-6 (lib. bdg. : alk. paper)
    1. Shipment of goods. I. Title. II. Title: Drop shipping.
HF5761.S34   1990
658.7'88—dc20   89–24324

British Library Cataloguing in Publication Data is available.

Library of Congress Catalog Card Number: 89–24324
ISBN: 0–89930–532–6

First published in 1990

Greenwood Press, Inc.
88 Post Road West, Westport, Connecticut 06881

Printed in the United States of America

The paper used in this book complies with the
Permanent Paper Standard issued by the National
Information Standards Organization (Z39.48–1984).

10 9 8 7 6 5 4 3 2 1

Contents

Illustrations

Preface

- A retail customer orders a TV set from a local appliance store. Shipment of the TV is made to the ultimate consumer from the regional warehouse of the manufacturer.
- A retailer purchases an inventory of products from a wholesaler. The order is sent by the wholesaler to the manufacturer who in turn ships the merchandise directly to the retail store.
- An individual orders a product from a mail order company; however, the manufacturer of the product ships the order directly to the ultimate consumer, using the preaddressed shipping label of the middleman.

All of these transactions are examples of drop shipping where products are sold for future delivery to a customer, while physical possession of the goods (inventory) bypasses the middleman.

Under traditional marketing methods, manufacturers sell to full-function middlemen who take possession of goods in anticipation of the inventory requirements necessary to supply the next level in the channel of distribution or the ultimate consumer. By taking possession of inventory, middlemen create time, place and information utilities for products by offering customers over-the-counter, off-the-shelf or immediate local delivery from inventory. Full-function middlemen accept the marketing risks incidental to physical possession of inventory. Inventories must be transported, financed, stored, protected, insured and displayed. Merchandise may become obsolete, stolen or damaged. All of these marketing risks related to holding inventory are incurred by full-function middlemen to offer immediacy within the marketplace. In other words, they want to have the right product in the right place at the right time to supply their customers.

The criteria for drop shipping involves the requirement that goods are sold for future delivery, while the possession of inventory bypasses a middleman. Many marketing textbooks equate drop shipping with a desk jobber or limited-function middleman. These middlemen are limited to the extent that they do not take possession of inventory. However, drop shipping is used by some of the most prestigious, full-function middlemen and manufacturers of both consumer and industrial products. The scope of drop shipping as a marketing function has been obscured by lack of data, since the dollar value of drop shipped orders lies hidden in the sales records of a wide variety of wholesalers, distributors and retailers.

Little has been written on the subject of drop shipping because the bulk of all products are sold through full-function middlemen who stock inventory. The major textbooks on marketing, wholesaling, retailing, transportation and distribution usually devote a few sentences to the subject of drop shipping, along with outdated definitions and concepts. Likewise, the dozens of books on mail order and direct marketing virtually ignore any reference to drop shipping, even though drop shipping is a natural adjunct to mail order marketing. Through direct marketing, products are sold for future delivery, and the function of filling orders can be shifted backward through the channel of distribution to the manufacturer or stocking distributor who will drop ship products. Under these circumstances, drop shipping may offer many advantages for the mail order dealer or distributor.

This book examines all facets of drop shipping as a marketing function. In an effort to reveal the marketing implications of drop shipping, this book will answer the following questions: Where and when can drop shipping function within the marketplace? What are the costs surrounding single-unit or small order drop shipments? How can transportation or logistical costs be affected by the use of drop shipping? Can drop shipping reduce, eliminate or shift the marketing costs and risks of manufacturers and middlemen? What are the advantages and disadvantages of drop shipping for the manufacturer, middleman and ultimate consumer?

Many other uses of drop shipping as a marketing function will be reviewed, along with the results of a survey directed to 400 companies that drop ship products for mail order firms. The interpretation of the survey results may offer manufacturers and middlemen guidelines for the formulation of marketing policies relative to drop shipping. Although drop shipping is used by many types of middlemen, mail order firms are perhaps in the best position to benefit from the use of drop shipping, and expanded information is provided specifically for them.

DROP SHIPPING AS A MARKETING FUNCTION

1

Drop Shipping: Definitions and Usage

TRADITIONAL MARKETING METHODS

Under ordinary circumstances, the majority of all manufacturers of both consumer and industrial products incur the risks of production, storage and credit, in addition to the sales and advertising costs necessary to gain wholesale distribution or to sell to the ultimate consumer. A functional middleman acts as an intermediary in business transactions between manufacturers or stocking entities and the succeeding levels in the channel of distribution to the end user or consumer. Most manufacturers of both consumer and industrial products prefer to sell to full-function middlemen who stock inventory of the products sold. These traditional methods of marketing products through full-function middlemen indicate that physical possession of inventory and title (ownership) flow hand in hand through the channel of distribution. By stocking products, full-function middlemen assume all of the marketing risks associated with the physical possession of inventory.

ORIGINS OF THE TERM

In the past, the term *drop shipment* has been used to describe inventory that physically bypasses a limited-function middleman who initiated the drop ship order and is shipped directly to the customer of the middleman by a manufacturer or stocking entity. A *limited-function middleman*, by definition, never has possession of inventory and is limited to the extent that this type of business entity does not stock inventory while performing all of the other marketing activities of a full-function middleman who stocks inventory. A limited-function middleman who initiates drop ship orders has also been defined in the past as a *drop shipper*, from an institutional standpoint. Both the limited-function middleman and drop shipper have also been defined as desk or parlor jobbers, implying that since these business entities do not incur the direct costs of stocking inventory, anyone with a desk, a parlor and presumably a typewriter and telephone can be a drop shipper.

Although past definitions of the terms drop shipping, drop shipment and drop shipper are relatively obscure, it is fairly obvious that the term *drop* refers to the manufacturer or stocking entity that physically performs the act of shipping products directly to the customer of a limited-function middleman. Under this interpretation, a drop shipper is a specific type of limited-function middleman who uses the services of a drop or stocking entity that ships products to the customer of the middleman.

However, if the drop or stocking entity is performing the act of shipping products to the customers of middlemen, it appears that the stocking entity that is providing drop shipping services should also be defined as the drop shipper from a marketing function standpoint, rather than defining a specific type of middleman. When a middleman places a purchase order with a supply source (manufacturer or stocking entity) for products to be held as inventory by a middleman, the supply source is the shipper (see, figure 1).

For purposes of this book, the drop shipper is defined as the stocking entity that performs drop shipping services as a marketing function by shipping products to the customers of the middleman who initiated the drop ship order (see figure 2). For those who prefer to continue to define a drop shipper from an institutional viewpoint, as the entity that initiates drop ship orders as a limited-function middleman (parlor or desk jobber), then the term drop shipper as used in this book can be defined as the drop (omitting shipper)—the supply source or stocking entity.

Limited-function middlemen would then be defined as a business entity that does not stock inventory and initiates drop ship orders. A full-function middleman that normally stocks inventory of all products sold can obviously initiate drop ship orders, but should not be redefined as a limited-function middleman.

PREVIOUS DROP SHIPPING STUDIES AND
CASE HISTORIES

There have been few, if any, readily available studies regarding drop shipping, although there have been brief references to drop shipping and the drop shipper in marketing textbooks for many years. The lack of information on the function of drop shipping has been based to a great extent

Figure 1
Physical Flow of Purchase Orders and Products Held as Inventory by Middlemen

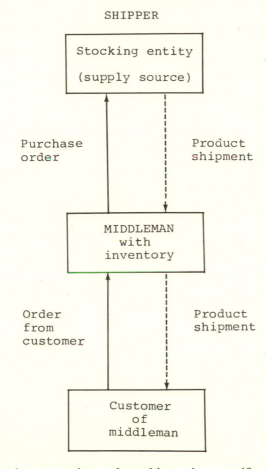

on the outdated concept that a drop shipper is a specific type of limited-function middleman, or a parlor or desk jobber of minor importance. This narrow concept of drop shipping is understandable since the role of drop shipping in the marketplace has only been measured in the past by incomplete data, regarding the activities of a very small group of limited-function middlemen. Most references to the role of drop shipping relate to the distribution of bulky products such as lumber, iron, steel, furniture, petroleum and coal and are confined to only a few lines of trade, in spite of the fact that there are economies to be gained by the elimination of the handling and storage of inventory by middlemen through the use of drop shipping.

As an example, one of the earliest references concerning drop shipping was described in the *Principles of Marketing* by Beckman and Maynard of

Figure 2
Physical Flow of Purchase Orders and Products Drop Shipped by the Stocking Entity

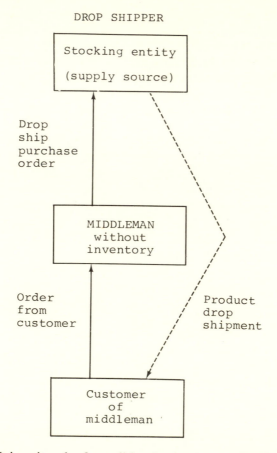

Ohio State University, the first edition having been published in 1927 and revised in 1946 as follows:

> On the basis of sales volume, the drop shipper or "desk jobber" is the most important limited-function wholesaler. He is so known because of the trade practice of referring to a shipment made directly from the factory to a retailer or industrial user as a "drop shipment." Drop shippers . . . have an office but no warehouse, since they do not take physical possession of the goods . . . they take title to the goods and assume responsibility for shipment. . . . In 1939 there was nearly 1,000 drop shippers with sales of 475 millions, . . . which constitutes less than 2% of all sales of full service and limited function wholesalers. About 90% of drop shippers operate in two lines of trade, coal and coke [in addition to] lumber and construction

materials . . . petroleum . . . farm products . . . and machinery. Since many costly functions are not performed by the drop shipper, his expenses are low, constituting but 6.4% of sales. . . . Drop shippers of lumber, for example, incur expenses of but 7.5% of sales while the expenses of regular wholesalers are 21% of their sales. The limit to the development of this business [as a drop shipper] is that most of it must be in carload lots or in original packages. Many manufacturers dislike the drop shipper and discourage his operations, for he tends to force certain functions back to the manufacturer, particularly that of storage and risk of obsolescence.[1]

Some thirteen years after the previous reference was published, *Wholesaling,* a book by Beckman, Engle, and Buzzell was published in 1959 with very similar definitions as follows:

Drop Shippers: The most important type of limited function wholesaler in terms of sales is the drop shipper or "desk jobber." In 1954 there were about 2,600 establishments operated by drop shippers, with total sales of approximately $2.2 billion. When a shipment of goods is made directly from the factory or to an industrial user on an order secured by a wholesaler and transmitted to the factory, it is generally known in the trade as a "drop shipment." Practically every wholesaler on occasion resorts to this practice, but when a wholesaler does the bulk of his business in that manner or fully specializes in such operations he is designated as a drop shipper, desk jobber, parlor wholesaler or direct mill supplier. The drop shipper usually operates from an office . . . maintains no warehouse . . . takes title to the goods . . . assumes all the risks incident to the ownership of such goods . . . in lines of trade where the goods are economically bulky. The differences in operating expenses between drop shippers and regular wholesalers are particular in merchandise such as lumber and building materials. In that line of trade, drop shippers in 1954 had a cost of doing business of 6.7 percent of net sales, while regular wholesalers of lumber and building materials with yards, operated at a cost of 12.5 percent.[2]

The same authors noted earlier, "One study made in the lumber and building materials industry indicated that in 1948, the cost of doing business of drop shippers was 5.4% of net sales, while regular lumber wholesalers, with yards, operated at costs of 14.0% of net sales. This indicates that drop shipping is especially valuable in reducing distribution costs in bulky lines such as lumber, iron, steel, furniture, petroleum, coal, vegetables and fruits."[3] Yet another author states: "The drop shipper performs all the functions of a regular wholesaler, except those of delivery and warehousing. He will make the sale and assume the credit function, but the manufacturer will assume responsibility for delivering the merchandise to the wholesaler's customer."[4]

Authorities on industrial marketing have also indicated:

In the industrial supplies, equipment and machinery trade, the only important type of limited-function wholesaler is the "drop shipper," who, like all wholesalers, buys and sells on his own account and performs other wholesaling functions but does not carry stocks (inventory of merchandise) or physically handle the goods in which he deals. . . . Most industrial distributors handle a certain portion of their sales on a drop shipment basis, but only when such methods of operation become the sole or the predominant method of doing business is the firm classified as a drop shipper. . . . Generally speaking, drop shipments are more common in the industrial field than in most consumer goods lines. This is due in part to the bulky nature of many equipment and machinery items and the consequent opportunities to reduce costs through the elimination of inventories on such sales and the rehandling operations incident to receiving, storing and order filling. . . . A survey of 126 general line wholesalers indicated that approximately 23% of their business was transacted as drop shipments.[5]

An authority on logistics offers the following definitions:

Drop shippers are limited-function wholesalers in that they seldom take physical possession of the goods. Commodities such as coal, lumber, construction materials, agricultural products, and heavy machinery are bulky and require the economies of shipment by carload lots. The drop shipper typically purchases the carload from the supplier in anticipation of a future order. Once a buyer is found, the drop shipper assumes the responsibility and ownership of shipment until it is accepted by the customer. Because no warehouse facilities are maintained, the drop shipper's risk of title bearing varies with the time lag between purchase and sale of the carload. Apart from the risk, he also incurs the risks and costs of credit extension and receivables collection. This distinction between the practice of drop shipping and the drop shipper is important. Drop shipping is the practice of shipping an order direct from the supplier to the customer, although a middleman might be involved in the transaction. For example, headquarters purchasing might centrally purchase a large quantity of bulk merchandise. Instead of requiring shipment to the firm's distribution warehouse, the company might allocate portions of the shipment directly to its retail stores. This practice is termed drop shipping. The drop shipper, on the other hand, is a distinct middleman who arranges for shipment, takes title, assumes responsibility for shipment and functions as a merchant middleman in the over-all distribution channel.[6]

Additional repetitive definitions have been indicated in virtually dozens of other texts, some of which negate the role of drop shipping. As an example, one marketing text indicates that:

> The drop shipper, also known as a "desk jobber" and as a "direct-mill shipper," has a relatively low cost of operation. In 1948, the latest year for which data are available, his costs were 4.4 percent of sales, as contrasted with 12.5 percent of all merchant wholesalers. To a large degree, this lower cost is a result of eliminating performance of the wholesale function. He does this by placing his orders with the manufacturers and having them ship direct to the retailer. Again, this practice does not necessarily mean a lower total cost of distribution, in fact, it is highly possible that the development of the drop shipper in many fields has resulted in higher distribution costs, because he forces storage back onto the manufacturer, who may not be able to provide this function as economically as a specialized wholesaler can. In addition, the cost of transportation may be considerably increased because of the smaller sized shipments the manufacturer must make to the retailer. Drop shippers increased rapidly from 1939 to 1948, when their number grew from 937 to 1,769 and their sales expanded from $475 million to $2,782 million. At the same time their cost of operation declined sharply from 6.4 percent of sales to 4.4 percent. Although drop shippers operate in various fields, such as farm products and petroleum, they are heavily concentrated in the sale of (1) lumber and construction materials and (2) coal and coke. These are fields to which their methods are ideally suited—merchandise is bulky, so that substantial savings can be achieved by the elimination of handling at the wholesale level, and retailers frequently purchase in carload lots. Where such conditions are not found—and they seldom are—drop shipping is not likely to grow; in brief, the potential field for drop shipping is a limited one.[7]

Other past definitions include: "Drop shipping. A process of eliminating one movement of goods. A manufacturer ships his goods directly to a retailer, bills the wholesaler who collects from the retailer. By this sytem, a saving is realized by omitting reshipping from wholesaler to retailer."[8] Another reference to drop shipping virtually duplicates the views of other authors:

> Drop Shippers: The drop shipper, also known as a desk jobber, takes title to the goods he sells but does not take physical possession. Orders that the drop shipper received from his customers are forwarded directly to the manufacturer who then ships the goods directly to the buyer. The buyer pays the drop shipper for the goods, and the drop shipper, in turn, pays the manufacturer. The drop shipper exists primarily in trades characterized by bulky commodities, such as lumber and building materials, coal and

some farm products. In these trades there are numerous opportunities for cost savings through the elimination of extra handling in transportation and storage, and customers of the drop shipper often purchase such bulky products in carload lots.[9]

Other reference books on various aspects of marketing have similar definitions as to the narrow usage of the terms related to drop shipping. In particular they refer to the drop shipper whom they clearly define as a specific type of limited-function middleman, which can only be described as an institutional, rather than a functional concept.

From a marketing standpoint, drop shipping has not been used by the desk or parlor jobber alone, since many well-established middlemen, who would ordinarily stock inventory of all products sold, may initiate drop ship orders. The total volume of business transacted on a drop ship basis on a national level has been grossly underestimated, based on the narrow view that drop shipping is an exclusive activity of limited-function middlemen. This estimate completely overlooks the vast number of drop shipping transactions that are initiated by full-function middlemen. In addition, many thousands of small mail order firms, wholesalers and jobbers do substantial business through drop shipping, however the sales volume of their drop shipped orders does not appear in governmental or trade association publications. Very few businesses reveal what percentage of their purchases were initiated as drop ship orders or which products were purchased to be stocked as inventory.

EXPANDED DEFINITIONS AS A MARKETING FUNCTION

From the few references on the subject of drop shipping, early writers concluded that a drop shipper is a limited-function middleman who does not take possession of the products sold, and sometime in the early marketing history of this country, drop shippers did the bulk of their business in very restricted product lines such as coal and lumber. This concept as to the definition of a drop shipper has appeared in various books on marketing, wholesaling and distribution in the past, and the same definition appears in reference books, year after year, without any reference to the origin of the definition or any modification for contemporary usage.

It appears that more meaningful definitions can be offered for the terms drop shipping, drop shipping services, drop ship, drop ship order or drop shipment, drop shipper and, to some extent, the definition of a limited-function middleman.

For purposes of this book, the following definitions are offered:

DROP SHIPPING: Drop shipping is a marketing function where physical possession of goods sold bypasses a middleman, while title flows through all those concerned. The function of drop shipping involves both the middleman who initiates the drop ship order and the stocking entity that provides drop shipping services by filling the order for the middleman.

DROP SHIPPING SERVICES: Drop shipping services are provided by the business entity that holds inventory of goods and fulfills the service by performing the act of shipping products to the customers of the entity that initiated the drop ship purchase order.

DROP SHIP: Drop ship refers to the performance of drop shipping services by the business entity that holds inventory. In other words, ''Will your firm drop ship for our company?'' is the same as asking the business firm that holds inventory whether they will provide drop shipping services.

DROP SHIP ORDER or DROP SHIPMENT: Both these terms are purchase orders for products that will be filled through the marketing function of drop shipping, initiated by one entity, a middleman, and performed by another, a stocking entity that holds inventory.

DROP SHIPPER: From a marketing standpoint, a drop shipper would more clearly be defined as any firm that holds inventory and provides drop shipping services for middlemen, because the physical act of filling orders is performed by the stocking entity or supply source that holds inventory and drop ships the product to the customer of the middleman.

LIMITED-FUNCTION MIDDLEMAN: A limited-function middleman never stocks inventory, but accepts orders for products from customers for future delivery and initiates drop ship orders that are filled by a stocking entity, supply source or drop shipper that provides drop shipping services. However, a full-function middleman that usually stocks inventory of all products sold can also initiate drop ship orders.

A firm that stocks inventory of products and performs the physical function of drop shipping products for middlemen is more clearly defined as the drop shipper. From a functional viewpoint, the entity that holds inventory is usually the manufacturer, a wholesaler or distributor, while the entity initiating the drop ship order can be either a limited- or full-function middleman defined as an importer, distributor, jobber, wholesaler or retailer. The function of filling orders is shifted backward through the channel of distribution by middlemen to the entity that holds inventory and provides drop shipping services. Drop shipping cannot exist in the marketplace unless a stocking entity agrees to ship goods to the customer of the middleman. The key to the performance of the function of drop shipping, therefore, lies with the firm that stocks products. A mail order company that sells at retail should be defined as such: a retailer, selling products for future delivery as a mail order firm, even if all of the products are drop shipped by another business entity that holds inventory.

Another indication of contemporary usage regarding the drop shipper concerns the fact that every known past and present drop ship directory, drop shipping source directory and directory of drop shippers lists manufacturers or middlemen that stock inventory and provide drop shipping services for middlemen. As in the past, if the drop shipper is defined as a desk or parlor jobber or a limited-function middleman, then a directory of drop shippers would contain the names and addresses of middlemen who initiate drop ship orders. There is no evidence that there are any directories that identify limited-function middlemen, parlor or desk jobbers as drop shippers, nor would there be any particular economic value in compiling such a list. The major role of drop shipping relates to the manufacturer or distributor who stocks inventory and performs the physical act of drop shipping products to the customers of the middlemen who initiate drop ship orders. The function of drop shipping cannot take place unless there are stocking entities willing to perform drop shipping services, and accordingly these entities should be defined as drop shippers from the standpoint of performing a marketing function, rather than as a specific type of middleman.

Drop shipping as a marketing function is used within this book in the broad sense of the definition of the term function. Webster's *New Collegiate Directory* indicates that a function is "one of a group of related actions, contributing to a larger action" or a "quality, trait or fact dependent and varying with another," while an action is "a thing accomplished over a period of time." Drop shipping defines the functional and dependent relationship between the business entity that initiates drop ship orders and the supply source that provides drop shipping services, which are related actions that take place over a period of time. In addition, the term function further removes drop shipping from the limited and institutionalized definition of a drop shipper as a specific type of middleman, desk or parlor jobber. Those in the academic world defining marketing functions in the rigid framework of buying, selling, storing, etc., may prefer to define drop shipping as a marketing method or policy, and both of these terms have been used in the title of this book, giving the reader a choice of concepts. Another example concerning the problem of definitions is indicated by the unresolved academic question as to whether or not marketing is a science. However, for the purposes of this book, the term marketing function in the broad sense best describes the role of drop shipping in the marketplace. It is also clear that a function can be contained in or be part of a larger function.

U.S. POSTAL SERVICE DEFINITION OF A DROP SHIPMENT

As an example of a definition of a drop shipment that is unrelated to usage as a marketing function, the U.S. Postal Service indicates the following definition in the "Glossary of Postal Terms," postal publication 32, April 1988: "Drop shipment—mailable items transported by the mailer, or picked up from the mailer by a nonpostal commercial carrier, transported to another city and mailed for delivery in or near the city of destination." As an example of Postal Service usage, a holder of a postal permit in New York ships a large quantity of bulk mail to Los Angeles where the out-of-state postal permit would be verified and the mail would be allowed to enter the postal system in Los Angeles. Express mail drop-ship allows an express mail overnight pouch to be opened by the post office at the destination of the pouch and the contents mailed locally. The term *drop* as used here, is the location where the mail enters the postal system and is mentioned only to indicate that there are a number of varied definitions of the same term.

TRANSPORTATION DEFINITIONS

The term drop shipping has sometimes been used to define split or alternate destination shipments. This definition does not involve merchandise bypassing a functional middleman, since shipment is made to a different location or branch of the very same company that ordered the product. As an example, the buying office of a department store may issue a purchase order to have a manufacturer ship products to ten different branches of their own retail outlets. Some would call this transaction a drop shipment, however this process is nothing more than a purchase order directing that merchandise be shipped to various locations. Since products are not shipped by the manufacturer to a retail customer of the store, the transaction is not a drop shipment from a marketing standpoint.

A similar trade usage of the term drop shipping relates to partial shipments or drop-off points. A retail lumber yard may have a truckload of orders for numerous customers. As the order for each customer is "dropped off" by the truck, some trade usage may define this delivery function as a drop shipment. This function would be more clearly defined as simply the delivery of products to multiple destinations from one delivery truck, rather than drop shipping.

In addition, the definition of drop shipping as a marketing function should not be confused with usage concerning the delivery of United Parcel Service (UPS) packages. While similar to the use of the term drop shipment as defined previously by the U.S. Postal Service, Todd Barr indicates in *Catalog Age* that drop shipping is sometimes called "zone skipping," and "in drop shipping, the packages to be shipped via UPS are transported (by line haul or motor freight) to a distant point called a drop point, where the UPS rates are lower for their destination, and then given to UPS for final delivery. The distant point usually corresponds to the UPS district service center."[10]

This function is similar to that performed by a freight forwarder or a freight or package consolidator, which as an example would ship truck loads of merchandise from New York to California. Upon arrival the packages would be delivered locally. The transportation economies of freight consolidators are obvious, however it is questionable as to whether these activities should be called drop shipments, as least from a marketing viewpoint. The study of freight forwarders and consolidators would be better left to books on transportation, distribution or freight handling systems. The marketing definition of drop shipping involves three entities: a middleman who accepts orders from customers and initiates the drop ship order, a manufacturer or stocking entity that drop ships the product, and the customer of the middleman who is to receive delivery of the product.

One transaction, however, might include both the marketing and transportation definitions of drop shipping. A mail order firm in New York might receive ten different orders for bulky desks from retail customers, all within the Denver, Colorado, area. The mail order firm then sends shipping labels and instructions to the manufacturer of the desks in Pennsylvania to have them drop ship each individual desk order to the customers of the middleman in Colorado. The manufacturer would then have a motor freight common carrier ship all ten desks to a freight consolidator or freight forwarder in Denver, which in turn has each desk reshipped by local truck to the customers of the mail order firm. The desk manufacturer in Pennsylvania is drop shipping the desks for the mail order firm (marketing definition), while the freight consolidator in Denver is drop shipping the desks for the manufacturer (transportation definition).

DROP SHIPPING VERSUS ORDER
FULFILLMENT SERVICES

Although the terms drop shipping and order fulfillment appear to have similar meanings and are often used interchangeably, there are differences. As mentioned, drop shipping as a marketing function involves three entities: (1) the ultimate consumer who has ordered a product for future delivery from the firm soliciting the order; (2) the firm that offers to sell products to the ultimate consumer and initiates the drop ship order; and (3) the stocking entity that holds inventory and drop ships the product to the customer. The relationship among all three entities involves the payment for the goods and the transfer of title (ownership). On the other hand, fulfillment services, as such, can be offered by an entity that holds inventory and fills orders with or without ownership of the product.

Order fulfillment services are often performed in cases where the ultimate consumer or the recipient of the shipment did not pay for the product. As an example, a firm may want to give baskets of fruit to their customers as gifts during a holiday season. They would be hard pressed to order half-bushel baskets of fruit from Florida and then reship the baskets to their gift recipients, particularly because of the perishability of the product. Instead, the firm would supply the fruit packer with a mailing list. The fruit packer is providing a fulfillment service by filling small or single-unit orders, and the recipients of the baskets did not order nor are they expected to pay for the fruit which is considered to be a gift. The fulfillment systems of the advertising specialty business which includes calendars, pens, ashtrays, and the tens of thousands of other items that are imprinted with an advertiser's name, are also given away free. The firm imprinting the products and shipping single units to recipients is providing a fulfillment service.

But how should the following transaction be defined? A bank gives a premium to depositors for opening a large account. The depositor selects a TV set as the premium in consideration for opening the account. The bank forwards the order to the regional warehouse of the TV manufacturer that handles premium fulfillment. Should this order be termed a drop shipment? Although this is a gray area, and the depositor did not buy the TV from the bank, there is a contract for fulfillment, because the bank has agreed to deliver the TV to the depositor in consideration for opening the account. In this case it does appear that the transaction can be defined as a drop shipment.

SEPARATE FULFILLMENT SERVICES

Direct marketers or any type of middleman for that matter that does not want to incur the costs of maintaining a warehouse or storage facilities or being involved with filling orders can contract for all of these services with a public warehouse or order fulfillment company. Fulfillment service firms do not have title to the products they store and handle. As an example, a large West Coast manufacturer of consumer appliances may contract with a warehouse on the East Coast to fill orders. Carload lots of appliances could be shipped to the East Coast warehouse that has agreed to provide storage and fulfillment services. When a retail store customer of the manufacturer orders a variety of appliances, the warehouse would ship the complete order to the customer of the manufacturer. If the manufacturer owned the warehouse, the same order fulfillment functions would be performed.

Since the business entity that is providing fulfillment services does not own the products under their name, the services provided are not drop shipments, but are fulfillment services that are performed based on the directions of the business entity that has title to the products. As an example, some fulfillment firms offer so many services that a direct marketer could have inventories of all products shipped to the fulfillment service company. The fulfillment company would provide racks or bins for the storage of the products, take monthly inventory, pick orders and prepare for shipment, type labels, insert invoices and ship the products. The client of the warehouse fulfillment service would pay a fixed percentage of billing or a flat price per item for total service that would be paid when orders are filled.

Other fulfillment firms offer a variety of services such as handling orders, packing, multiunit packing, shipping against documents, handling self-liquidators, coupon redemption and shipping parcel post, UPS or motor freight. In addition to order fulfillment of single-unit orders, the firm will receive merchandise to be stored and will break down master cartons into individual units. Order processing services may include opening mail, removing contents, typing labels, sorting labels by zones, affixing labels to cartons and shipping the products. If there is a requirement to handle money, a special account for each program is established, in addition to having facilities for invoicing and handling customer returns or refunds.

Some fulfillment firms offer more technical and detailed services such as on-line order entry; on-line zip code file; tape-to-disk and electronic data interchange order entry system; order price sequencing by order number; UPS delivery zone or zip codes; picking sheets by item; ID or order number to facilitate picking and packing; order inquiries including order number, customer name, zip code, phone number and item number. In addition the firm may provide order transaction history; the sales offer; catalog or source code processing and reporting; multiple catalog or multiple item pricing; item quantity break pricing; accounts receivable system; mailing list systems with disk-to-tape options; inventory control systems; alternate items; purchase order systems; physical inventory systems; comprehensive sales analysis systems; order refund systems; operator productivity reports; on-line documentation systems with definition options; integrated multilevel operator security systems, bar coding, point of sales and UPS manifest systems. Through the use of the facilities and services of fulfillment companies, virtually all storage, order fulfillment and accounting functions can be shifted to another firm on a contract basis by the firm that has title to the products. The use of such fulfillment services, performed by another company, may or may not be cost effective for the client of the fulfillment company.

PRODUCT CLASSIFICATIONS

In theory, virtually any type of product can be distributed through drop shipping as long as the future delivery of goods is acceptable to all parties concerned. If both the stocking entity and middleman mutually agree to a drop shipping arrangement, there is also the assumption that the costs of order handling and shipping are not prohibitive. A costly order for one firm may be profitable for another, since there are numerous variables:

price of the product, markups, weight, shipping costs and order processing costs.

DROP SHIPPING: CONSUMER PRODUCTS

As long as a product can be sold for future delivery, there is the possibility that the product can be drop shipped by a stocking entity. It is unlikely that a package of chewing gum would be drop shipped by a manufacturer to the ultimate retail consumer, however it is possible that a large shipment of multiple cases of gum could be drop shipped from the regional warehouse of the manufacturer to a grocery chain, as a service to a wholesaler. Since the vast majority of all consumer goods are sold by retail stores that stock inventory and sell over-the-counter, drop shipping cannot take place for these transactions.

DROP SHIPPING: INDUSTRIAL PRODUCTS

Many manufacturers of industrial products offer drop shipping services for their distributors, wholesalers and jobbers. Product classifications may include a wide variety of raw materials, supplies, equipment and machinery. The concept of drop shipping is quite compatible with industrial product distribution because these middlemen usually do not stock every size and type of item they may distribute for their product sources. Most industrial product end users are accustomed to delay in delivery which could allow the products to be drop shipped directly from the manufacturer, rather than from an inventory held by an industrial products middleman. It would be difficult to document the vast number and dollar value of industrial products that are distributed through drop shipping, since these data usually lie hidden in the records of private business transactions between the supplier and middleman.

TYPES OF MIDDLEMEN

As stated earlier, any type of middleman (retailer, wholesaler, distributor or jobber) can initiate drop ship orders, as long as the entity that stocks inventory is willing to provide drop shipping services. Limited-function middlemen, according to marketing textbooks, never stock inventory and deal exclusively in drop shipping. Full-function middlemen who would normally stock inventories of all products sold can also initiate orders to be drop shipped by a manufacturer or other stocking entity. Of particular interest are mail order firms that always sell products for future delivery, and this type of middleman is perhaps in the best position to profitably use the function of drop shipping as a marketing policy.

USAGE BY VARIOUS INDUSTRIES

Appliance Retailing

Several of the largest U.S. manufacturers of major appliances including stoves, refrigerators, air conditioners and TVs have used drop shipping involving a merchandise "display plan," with subsequent delivery of the product to the retail customers of their appliance dealers. The regional distribution center of the manufacturer supplies the appliance retailers with display samples, but the dealer does not carry any inventory of these products. Because shipment of individual appliance orders is made directly from the warehouse stock of the manufacturer to the retail consumer, the appliance dealer avoids the costs of financing inventory, however they cannot earn the quantity discounts which would normally be offered by the manufacturer. The drop shipping arrangement aids in solving a number of problems associated with appliance retailing: lack of adequate capital, inventory control, service, delivery, installation and obsolete goods. The appliance dealer eliminates the cost of warehouse space, delivery trucks and driver salaries, damaged goods, markdowns, and interest on working capital. Even though the retailer must pay single lot prices, the cost savings gained by the elimination of the problems of stocking inventory offsets the disadvantage of not earning larger quantity discounts from the manufacturer. This same type of drop shipping program is offered by furniture, farm equipment and many other types of manufacturers.

As an example of factory direct drop shipping in the appliance industry, the president of a co-op apartment in New York City performed the basic research for the purchase of fifty-one replacement through-the-wall air conditioners and sleeves. Quotations were obtained from three dealers, and one offered substantially lower prices than the others. A deposit check and the order, which was well over $20,000, was sent to the low bidder. Several weeks later the complete shipment was delivered by motor freight to the front of the apartment building, directly from the factory of the air conditioner manufacturer in San Antonio, Texas. The dealer stated that they could not spare one of their own employees to supervise the unloading and verification of the order. However, the regional sales manager of the manufacturer was available, verified the delivery and received a certified check for the balance due, which was made payable to the dealer. The only involvement of the air conditioner dealer was to submit the quotation, accept the order and deposit, order the items from the manufacturer and receive the check for the balance due on delivery from the factory representative of the manufacturer. The air conditioner dealer never took possession of the products, and the transaction was a classic example of the use of drop shipping by an appliance retailer.

Mail Order Marine Equipment

Late in the 1970s, a catalog mail order firm was founded in the Southeast, with start-up costs of about $10,000. The products consisted of marine electronic products for small-boat owners and included items such as radar, depth finders, fish locators, ship-to-shore radios, and a large selection of other boat-related products. After several years the firm was grossing almost $1 million yearly, had four employees, toll free 800 numbers and an average sale of over $500 per customer. None of the merchandise was kept in inventory, and all products were drop shipped by the manufacturer or stocking distributor. The firm ran space ads in boating and sports magazines to generate inquiries for their four-color catalog of over thirty pages. Direct mail was also sent to known boat owners. Discounts of up to 40 percent off the suggested retail prices were offered to customers, and it was found that, by use of credit cards, factory-sealed cartons and fast UPS delivery from the firms providing drop shipping services, the mail order firm could compete on a national basis. Without the use of drop shipping as a marketing policy the firm could not have been formed with such small capitalization and have the low overhead costs that allowed substantial discounts to customers.

BUSINESS FORMS: SYNDICATED CATALOG

A division of a major producer of imprinted business forms offers dealers a drop shipping program through a syndicated catalog. The product line includes sales books, invoices, statements, bookkeeping systems, purchase orders, letterhead, business cards, mailing labels, envelopes, tax forms, one-write payroll systems and other products. Virtually all of the products are custom imprinted with the name and address of the customer of the dealer, and the manufacturer drop ships the orders directly to the end user under the shipping label of the dealer. The products are competitively priced, and the manufacturer offers a 30 percent discount off the preprinted retail prices in the catalog on all orders and reorders. The customers of the dealer add a flat 7 percent to the retail price of the order to cover shipping and handling costs. The syndicated catalog consists of forty pages, 8 1/2 x 11 inches, saddle stitched, printed on coated stock, and all pages have either full-color photos or color tints. The name and address of the dealer is printed on the front cover of the catalog and a bound-in order form and return envelope is included for use by the customer of the dealer. The custom imprinted catalogs are supplied for 25 cents each in quantities as low as fifty. The catalog is updated every three months, and the supplier offers the services of factory-trained representatives to assist in order placement via toll-free 800 numbers or FAX. All orders are processed in six days, and the dealer is billed for the orders on open account. At a cost of $250 per thousand, which amounts to 40,000 printed pages, the catalog provides dealers with a very cost effective means for promoting imprinted forms through direct mail or by distributing the catalogs to customers.

Medical Products

In certain industries, the function of drop shipping plays a vital role. A medical supply company that distributes products to testing laboratories or hospitals may sell products of manufacturers that are made from blood or other biologicals that may require proper refrigeration at all times. These types of products require special handling and storage and shipping precautions to protect the "integrity of the product." If a medical laboratory or hospital receives damaged or contaminated products, the problem can be resolved directly with the manufacturer, rather than the distributor. The manufacturer of such medical products could sell directly to testing laboratories or hospitals, however the medical product distributor provides a vital sales and marketing link between the manufacturer and end user. Because of the nature of these medical products, virtually all such items are drop shipped by the prime manufacturer directly to the customers of the distributor. Drop shipping may also be necessary when dealing with other products that are toxic, hazardous, perishable or may require special handling, shipping or packaging.

SCOPE OF THE SUBJECT

Based on the definitions of the various facets of drop shipping as a marketing function, it is evident that a wide variety of manufacturers and middlemen, including wholesalers, importers, distributors, jobbers and other stocking entities, can provide drop shipping services. In addition, a wide variety of consumer products and an equally diverse list of nonconsumer products are available on a drop ship basis. Middlemen who initiate drop ship orders include importers, jobbers, distributors, wholesalers and retailers of both consumer and industrial products. The study of drop shipping as a marketing function is elusive. There are no known sources of reliable statistical data that indicate the total dollar volume of business transactions designated as drop shipments or the types of middlemen or products involved. The sales records of tens of thousands of businesses contain the dollar value of drop shipped orders, however the volume of business transacted as drop shipped orders is usually not available separately.

As a example, a wholesaler of consumer products may stock inventory of most of the products sold, and the balance of sales made through the function of drop shipping, via the services of various manufacturers. On the other hand, a manufacturer of consumer or industrial products may only sell to middlemen who stock inventory and are never involved in drop shipping. Marketing research studies would have to be performed that would include surveys of a massive number of manufacturers and middlemen, covering virtually every type of consumer and industrial product, in an attempt to gain meaningful statistics as to the volume of sales transacted through the function of drop shipping, segmented by the type of product, source, middlemen and channel of distribution. It is acknowledged that the volume of business transacted as drop shipments in the marketplace is unknown and considered to be small, compared to the sales volume of products sold through middlemen who stock inventory at every successive level in the channel of distribution.

This book has been directed to mail order marketing methods and consumer products mainly because all mail order sales are made for future delivery. That's the basic criteria required for drop shipping to function, although drop shipped orders can be based on sales methods other than mail order. As an example, the purchasing agent of a manufacturer orders a special rivet gun from a distributor of industrial products. The order could have been placed in person, by written purchase order or by telephone. The industrial distributor does not have the product in stock and initiates a drop ship order for the product to be shipped by the producer of the rivet gun directly to the customer of the industrial distributor. Tens of thousands of similar transactions that involve building materials, industrial machinery, raw materials, office equipment and hundreds of other classifications of nonconsumer products do not involve conventional mail order sales methods. However, if the industrial distributor produces a mail order catalog or distributes catalog sheets and uses the drop shipping services of a supply source that stocks inventory of the products sold, at least from a functional standpoint, the marketing methods of the industrial distributor are no different from those of a mail order firm selling consumer goods. Since many of the same factors that relate to drop shipping apply equally to both consumer and industrial products, the classification of an industrial product could be substituted for references to consumer products, where applicable throughout this book.

EXPANSIVE ROLE OF DROP SHIPPING

In the past, drop shipping has been related to limited-function middlemen. This concept institutionalizes drop shipping and ignores the fact that drop ship orders can be initiated by a wide variety of full-function middlemen who usually stock inventory and include distributors, contractors, wholesalers, jobbers and retailers. Likewise, drop shipping services are being offered by vast numbers of manufacturers and stocking distributors, involving an extensive list of products. Many volumes could be filled with examples of the use of drop shipping by numerous manufacturers and middlemen, along with the thousands of drop shipping transactions that take place yearly. The case histories of the product groups mentioned in this chapter hardly scratch the surface as to the use of drop shipping as a marketing function.

NOTES

1. Theodore N. Beckman and Harold H. Maynard, *Principles of Marketing*, 4th ed. (New York: Ronald Press Company, 1946), pp. 289–290.

2. Theodore N. Beckman, Nathanael H. Engle, and Robert D. Buzzell, *Wholesaling*, 3rd ed. (New York: Ronald Press Company, 1959), pp. 169–170.

3. Theodore N. Beckman, and Nathanael H. Engle, *Wholesaling* (New York: Ronald Press Company, 1951), p. 218.

4. Douglas Banning, *Techniques for Marketing New Products* (New York: McGraw-Hill Book Company, 1957), p. 63.

5. Robert D. Buzzell, "Value Added by Industrial Distributors and Their Productivity" (Bureau of Business Research Monograph 96, College of Commerce and Administration, The Ohio State University, Columbus, OH, 1959), pp. 26–27.

6. Donald J. Bowersox, *Logistical Management* (New York: Macmillan Publishing Company, 1974), pp. 68–69.

7. Charles F. Phillips and Delbert J. Duncan, *Marketing Principles and Methods*, 6th ed. (Homewood, IL: Richard D. Irwin, Inc., 1968), pp. 342–343.

8. Stanley Strand, *Marketing Dictionary* (New York: Philosophical Library, Inc., 1962), p. 225.

9. Harry A. Lipson and John R. Darling, *Introduction to Marketing* (New York: John Wiley & Sons, Inc., 1971), p. 130.

10. Todd Barr, "UPS Drop Shipping Is for Everyone," *Catalog Age*, July 1987, p. 155.

2

Drop Shipping as a Marketing Policy

THE MARKETING RISKS OF HOLDING INVENTORY

Drop shipping exists as a marketing function due to choice or necessity. A manufacturer may have to drop ship products because of the position of the company in the market, trade practices, as a cost-reduction measure, to increase profits or as a service to middlemen. Middlemen, on the other hand, may deal in drop shipments to reduce costs or investment in inventory. The physical possession of inventory involves costs. The longer goods are held by either the manufacturer or middlemen, the greater are cumulative costs of possession.

If a manufacturer or other stocking entity provides drop shipping services for middlemen, the costs and risks of inventory possession are retained by the manufacturer, rather than being shifted to middlemen who would ordinarily stock inventory. All manufacturers could, as a matter of marketing policy, require every middleman to stock inventory and, by doing so, refuse to provide drop shipping services. However, the function of providing drop shipping services by the manufacturer does exist in the marketplace, indicating that there are advantages to the stocking entity regarding this marketing policy. The actual costs of holding inventory, which may include storage, insurance, personnel, protection, rent and order handling, along with the financial costs of stocking products, can be reduced or shifted, but they cannot be eliminated.

Once inventory is transferred to a middleman, all of the costs related to inventory are also shifted from the manufacturer to the next level in the channel of distribution. However, the manufacturer must still have all the facilities necessary to stock sufficient inventory to supply the future orders of middleman. Therefore, the costs of inventory maintenance continue to be incurred by both the manufacturer and full-function middlemen. If both the manufacturer and stocking middleman are to remain profitable, the total cumulative costs and risks of holding inventory must be passed on to the ultimate consumer. In a sense, the stocking middleman duplicates a share of the costs of holding inventory that was previously incurred by the manufacturer.

SHIFTING INVENTORY COSTS AND RISKS

If a middleman does not stock inventory, all of the direct costs and risks associated with inventory maintenance would be eliminated at this level in the channel of distribution. The middleman does not have to rent or finance storage facilities, pay the wages of warehouse personnel, taxes and insurance on storage space and numerous other costs associated with the physical possession of inventory. If the middleman uses the drop shipping services of a manufacturer or stocking distributor, these direct overhead costs are incurred by the entity holding inventory.

The costs and risks of holding inventory can be viewed from several perspectives. If a manufacturer ships merchandise to a middleman, the direct costs of holding inventory are also shifted to the middleman. If a manufacturer fills orders as drop shipments from an inventory that would ordinarily be held by a full-function middleman, then the manufacturer is performing as a middleman as far as holding inventory is concerned. Whether holding inventory and its associated costs are retained by the manufacturer, or shifted backward through the channel of distribution by the middleman to the manufacturer, the net result is the same regarding drop shipments.

Although the direct costs of holding inventory may be reduced or eliminated by a middleman who uses the drop shipping services of a manufacturer, the middleman may still incur hidden indirect costs. For providing drop shipping services, a manufacturer may charge a higher unit price for a product that is drop shipped for a middleman. In effect the middleman may be paying the stocking entity for overhead costs the middleman might have incurred had the middleman stocked the product and shipped from inventory. However, any overhead costs incurred indirectly by middlemen in the form of higher product prices on drop shipped orders may be lower when compared to the direct overhead costs of middlemen that stock inventory of the same products.

POLICY DECISION OF THE STOCKING ENTITY

Under traditional marketing methods, physical possession of inventory and title flow hand in hand through the channel of distribution. Most firms that hold inventory would prefer to sell to full-function middlemen and shift the marketing risks associated with inventory to the next level in the distribution channel. There are circumstances that may favor the offering of drop shipping services for middlemen by the stocking entity, as a matter of marketing policy.

A manufacturer selling products to full-function middlemen may require substantial financial resources to produce goods in sufficient quantity to fill the channel of distribution. While the risks of physical possession may be shifted to middlemen who stock inventory, the supplier may still have to wait thirty days or more for payment. In effect, the manufacturer is "lending" inventory to middlemen, with the expectation that payment will be forthcoming under the terms of sale. The manufacturer also has the basic marketing costs of selling to distributors or middlemen, which may take the form of compensation to salespeople and trade advertising. Manufacturers usually must also make expenditures on consumer advertising to stimulate demand for products in an effort to pull the product through the channel of distribution. By offering drop shipping services for middlemen, the stocking entity may find that there are some cost savings by centralizing inventory which is drawn upon by middlemen as drop shipments.

The policy decision to offer drop shipping services by a manufacturer may be based on the attitude of management toward the handling of small or single-unit orders. One watch manufacturer may offer a full drop shipping program with ample dealer aids, while another watch company, with the same or similar marketing costs, will not provide drop shipping services and only sell to middlemen who stock the merchandise in quantity. One firm favors drop shipping as a part of their marketing program, and the other may consider the service to be too much trouble, so "why bother" with drop shipping.

The decision to offer drop shipping services should be based on the objective to maximize profits. While drop shipping cannot be utilized by every manufacturer or stocking distributor, depending on the type of product, prices, shipping costs and other variables, some of the factors that could influence a decision to offer drop shipping services are as follows:

1. Will the time lapse between the acceptance of the order and shipment be satisfactory to all parties?

2. Is the product packaged in single-unit mailers or in unbroken lots that can be drop shipped without costly order handling?

3. Is the markup or wholesale price large enough to justify the handling of a single unit or small quantity?

4. Can smaller-than-usual discounts be extended to middlemen to cover any additional costs that may be involved?

5. Can efficient methods be developed for order handling and shipping the products?

6. Can drop shipping services be offered to all middlemen alike in order to meet governmental regulations?

7. Will the offering of drop shipping services increase sales and profits?

8. Can more advertising and promotion costs be shifted to middlemen by providing drop shipping services?

9. Can cash-with-order terms be required on drop shipments, as opposed to trade terms which would ordinarily be extended to middlemen who stock inventory?

POLICY DECISION OF THE MIDDLEMAN

Usually, full-function middlemen make purchases and take possession of inventory in anticipation of sales. Obviously, products must eventually flow from the producer to the end user. The middleman assumes the cost of inventory, in addition to all the marketing costs and risks required to sell to the next level in the channel of distribution or at retail. In many instances, the inventory control and investment problems of the middleman can be critical. If a middleman stocks merchandise that cannot be sold, there is the risk of having distress merchandise on hand. The retailer or middleman may call on the manufacturer to accept the return of the merchandise or to supply various types of financial support to aid in selling the products. Middlemen with adequate finances and storage facilities would usually prefer to stock all merchandise, however middlemen should consider the following factors regarding the use of drop shipping as a marketing policy:

1. Can the products be sold for future delivery?

2. Will the cost of paperwork or order processing be too great?

3. Will drop shipping produce cost savings based on alternate use of capital?

4. Can the cost of warehousing and order handling be reduced?

5. Will freight or transportation costs be lowered?

6. Can lower prices on products be offered to customers by use of the drop shipping services provided by the stocking sources of supply?

7. Can greater expenditures be made on advertising and selling functions through the use of drop shipping?

8. Can a larger line of products be offered to customers through drop shipping?

LEGAL ASPECTS: FTC MAIL ORDER RULE

A good portion of drop shipping involves mail order firms that deal with a manufacturer or stocking distributor that has agreed to drop ship products for the mail order firm. Once a mail order firm solicits business and a retail consumer orders a product, the "30 Day Mail Order Rule" comes into effect. Since the retail mail order customer has no knowledge of or contact with the supply source that drop ships the product, compliance with the "30 Day Mail Order Rule" is the full responsibility of the mail order dealer that sells to retail consumers. The product must be shipped within thirty days, or the customer has to be notified by the middleman regarding any delays.

If the manufacturer, as an example, fails to drop ship the merchandise within thirty days, the middleman who initiated the order is in violation of the Mail Order Rule. A portion of a written contract between the middleman and product source that is providing drop shipping services could state that orders would be filled within a specific length of time, and the supply source would notify the middleman as to the date the merchandise was shipped. The letters from the Federal Trade Commission, reproduced here, indicate that the relationship between the middleman initiating the drop ship orders and the stocking entity that fills the order is one of a private contract.

FEDERAL TRADE COMMISSION

Washington, DC 20580

Bureau of
Consumer Protection

May 27, 1983

Mr. Nicholas T. Scheel
Consolidated Marketing Services, Inc.
P.O. Box 1361
New York, New York 10017

Dear Mr. Scheel:

Thank you for your letter of March 9, 1983, requesting a staff opinion on mail order "drop-shipping."

A drop-shipping arrangement between a middleman and a manufacturer may, under certain conditions, be construed as "mail order" within the scope of the Mail Order Rule, depending on whether or not certain criteria and definitions are met.

First, the Rule is quite specific that the seller must "solicit" the buyer. Did the middleman approach the manufacturer and propose a drop-shipping arrangement wherein the middleman does the advertising and receives the orders from consumers, the middleman has solicited the manufacturer and the resulting drop-shipping activities cannot be defined as mail order between the two firms. The only mail order that exists in such a set of circumstances is the transaction between the consumer and the middleman. Any arrangement between the middleman and the manufacturer under these conditions is strictly a matter of private contract, enforceable by the courts.

Second, the order from the buyer to the seller must be "through the mails." If the order is placed by telephone, handed to the seller by private messenger service or transmitted electronically, it is not considered mail order.

Third, the Rule states that the seller must have "receipt of a properly completed order" as defined in Sec. 435.2(b) of the Rule.

Where a contract exists between a middleman and a manufacturer such that the manufacturer is responsible for sending delay option notices to the consumer (rather than the middleman sending the notices as would otherwise be the practice), and if the manufacturer fails to send such notices, then the middleman still remains responsible to the consumer in accordance with the Mail Order Rule. This is especially true since the middleman should be aware of the manufacturer's failure to send the merchandise and/or the delay option notices as per the contract. However, the manufacturer may have violated the terms of the business-to-business contract and may be privately sued by the middleman. Further, the Commission may decide to pursue an action against both firms since the manufacturer has primary responsibility under the contract

Please be advised that the above reflects staff opinion and is not considered binding on the Commission.

Thank you for contacting the Commission. Should you have further questions regarding mail order, please contact Raymond L. Rhine, Program Advisor for Mail Order Rule Enforcement at (202) 376–2891.

Very truly yours
Steve Ecklund
Legal Technician
Division of Enforcement

*   *   *

FEDERAL TRADE COMMISSION

Washington, D.C. 20580

Bureau of
Consumer Protection

August 9, 1983

Mr. Nicholas T. Scheel
Consolidated Marketing Services, Inc.
P.O. Box 1361
New York, NY 10017

Dear Mr. Scheel:

Thank you for your letter of June 6, 1983, requesting further clarification of the FTC staff's views on mail order "drop shipping."

Essentially, our position is that a "trade inquiry" is an inquiry to initiate specific negotiations for a private contract between two parties, as opposed to the general offering of a product in a solicitation to the public in general. Any response by a manufacturer to the middleman's trade inquiry is consequently part of the private contract process and should not be construed as a "solicitation" within the purview of the Mail Order Rule.

We feel that the term "solicitation" must be understood in the context of the Statement of Basis and Purpose of the Mail Order Rule. Because the Statement does not specifically address the issues of drop shipping or negotiated contracts, any meaning relating to these subjects must be interpreted from the Rule and Statement of Basis and Purpose. In Chapter V, Section C.3 of the Statement of Basis and Purpose . . . the implication is clear that the type of mail order referred to in the Rule between two businesses is understood to be of the same type as that between a business and a non-business consumer. Therefore, it is my opinion that since private negotiations and specific contractual arrangements between two businesses for a series of transactions which are intended to or do occur on a continuing basis are not of a non-business variety, they are not covered by the Rule.

The distinction between this on-going form of specific contract and the general contract into which a consumer enters during the course of routine mail order solicitation lies at the crux of the issue. We interpret the Mail Order Rule to apply only to consumer mail orders in response to a general offer (or solicitation) to the public, and not to continuing, privately negotiated contracts. As indicated in my May 27 letter, the middleman as the advertiser still remains responsible to the consumer in accordance with the Mail Order Rule, regardless of any arrangements between the middleman and the manufacturer. This is especially true since the middleman is responsible for and should be aware of any failure by the manufacturer to drop ship the merchandise and/or send the delay option notices if this is called for by the contract. Of course, if the manufacturer has violated the terms of the business-to-business contract, he may be privately sued by the middleman. Further, the Commission may decide to pursue an action against the manufacturer where it may have primary responsibility for complying with the Rule under the contract and it appears that unfair practices may be involved under Section 5 of the Federal Trade Commission Act.

We recognize that the Mail Order Rule and its Statement of Basis and Purpose do not and they cannot directly address all possibilities and permutations of possible relevance.

Please be advised that the above reflects staff opinion and is not considered binding upon the Commission.

> Very truly yours,
> Steve Ecklund
> Legal Technician
> Division of Enforcement

*　*　*

As of August 1989, the following clarification and update was received from Raymond L. Rhine, attorney for the Division of Enforcement, Federal Trade Commission, Bureau of Consumer Protection:

> The Federal Trade Commission's Mail Order Rule covers specifically merchandise "ordered by the buyer through the mails" which, in our view, includes the U.S. Postal Service as well as all of the private common carrier mail handlers. The method of shipment of orders placed by mail is generally irrelevant to any mail order rule provision. The shipment time requirements of the mail order rule [Rule Sec. 435.1(a)(1)] are applicable primarily to the company soliciting the sale regardless of the method of shipment used, as explained further in Mr. Ecklund's letter. The company should physically turn over any merchandise to whatever carrier they elect to use, in time to meet the Rule's requirements, i.e., the time stated in the solicitation or 30 days from receipt of a properly completed order if not time period is stated in the solicitation.

> Although the Commission is presently considering whether to amend the Mail Order Rule to cover telephone transactions, orders called in by

telephone with payment made by credit card are not now covered by the Rule. Although such transactions may not be covered by the Commission's Mail Order Rule, they are subject to general requirements of Section 5 of the Federal Trade Commission Act, which provides that "unfair and deceptive acts and practices" are illegal. If an order is placed by telephone and payment is made by a credit card number or a check sent through the mail, then the sale would be covered by the Rule.

Please note that the above is staff opinion only and should not be considered binding upon the Commission. If you have further questions, please feel free to contact me at (202) 326–2973.

Further information can be obtained from the FTC, regarding the basic document on the subject: Title 16, Commercial Practices, Rules and Regulations, Chapter I, Federal Trade Commission, Part 435, Mail Order Merchandise, November 5, 1975, as amended.

From all indications drop shipping may reduce the costs of middlemen who initiate drop ship orders. Full-function middlemen who stock inventory in addition to dealing in drop shipments may not be able to isolate the cost savings on drop shipments, and if the cost savings are passed on to customers, direct costs of drop shipments may not be fully covered.

Pricing policy under drop shipments should be guided by the Robinson-Patman Act, and lower prices based on cost savings be passed on to all customers equally. A manufacturer or stocking entity that only drop ships for special customers or as a favor, without extending the same service to all of their customers, may be dealing in preferential treatment which may be a violation of governmental regulations.

MARKETING POLICIES CAN MODIFY COSTS AND RISKS

All of the marketing costs and risks of the physical possession of goods are incurred by the entity that holds inventory. The marketing policy decision of a middleman to initiate drop ship orders depends on whether the product can be sold for future delivery and whether there is a manufacturer or stocking entity that is willing to provide drop shipping services. There is no doubt that drop shipping can eliminate or reduce the direct marketing costs for middlemen regarding the holding of inventory. But how much are the cost reductions? Through drop shipping, the middleman can never have too much or too little inventory; there is no possibility of having distress merchandise; and all of the direct costs regarding the storage, handling, order filling, protection and insurance are eliminated, since the stocking entity is not only retaining all the risks of holding inventory but providing drop shipping services as well.

On the other hand, a manufacturer or stocking entity that provides drop shipping services is holding an inventory that would normally be transferred, usually in quantity, to a full-function middleman. The stocking entity that agrees to provide drop shipping services can benefit by increasing business, as a service to middlemen, and charging higher prices on single-unit drop shipped orders, rather than offering quantity discounts that would normally be passed on to stocking middlemen. Drop shipping transactions involve two entities: the manufacturer or stocking distributor and a middleman who initiates drop ship orders. The function of drop shipping does exist, indicating that a marketing policy decision to deal in drop shipments has met the approval of tens of thousands of middlemen and manufacturers alike.

The benefits gained through the use of drop shipping as a marketing function may vary from one company to another, based on the types of products involved, the channel of distribution, the price of the merchandise, shipping costs and a variety of other factors.

3

Drop Shipping Research

"DROP SHIPPING AS A MEANS FOR REDUCING MARKETING COSTS"

There appear to be logical reasons why the function of drop shipping exists in the marketplace. It also seems logical that a hypothesis should first be established in reference to drop shipping as a means for reducing marketing costs, prior to any analysis of the reasons why firms deal in drop shipping. Another similar hypothesis could assume that drop shipping may reduce marketing costs of both the middleman and the stocking entity when the cost of handling small orders is not prohibitive. Some of the obvious marketing cost reduction aspects of drop shipping concern the facts that the middleman does not have to invest in inventory, and there is the elimination of the double handling of goods, while the stocking entity may have reduced costs in selling to middlemen and can offer centralized inventories to be drawn against by middlemen as drop shipments.

HANDLING SMALL ORDERS

The use of drop shipping as a marketing policy appears to be based on a balance of advantages and disadvantages. The cost reduction benefits for the stocking entity may be offset by the cost of handling less profitable small orders. Although a manufacturer who provides drop shipping services usually handles single-unit orders, the costs should be linked to the service provided middlemen. The definition of a costly small order would vary from one manufacturer to another and depend on the types of products, dollar value of the order, quantities and markup. A costly small or single-unit drop shipment for one manufacturer may be profitable for another.

The high potential cost of handling small orders by a manufacturer may create a problem whether the company sells to full-function middlemen who stock the product or handles drop shipments. As an example, a manufacturer who sells to stocking wholesalers may be willing to ship a single unit of the product to the wholesaler. The same single unit order could just as easily have been shipped directly to the customer of the wholesaler as a drop shipment. However, the manufacturer may have established that an unbroken carton of twelve units of the product would be the minimum quantity that could be sold to a stocking wholesaler, based on the costs involved. Likewise, the twelve-unit quantity may be the minimum order that could be drop shipped profitably, and any smaller order would be unacceptable as being too costly.

If a manufacturer or stocking entity agrees to drop ship single units of a product, this type of order no doubt has already been established as being profitable, therefore the problems concerning the handling of such orders are eliminated from the hypothesis. An attempt should be made to investigate the advantages and disadvantages of drop shipping as a marketing function, rather than to establish what size or dollar value of an order is profitable from a cost accounting viewpoint. Since marketing includes all functions that facilitate the movement of goods from producer to consumer, drop shipping is one of these functions.

SURVEY OF MANUFACTURERS WHO DROP SHIP FOR MAIL ORDER DEALERS

In order to study drop shipping, a method of marketing must be selected where physical possession of goods need not be transferred at the time of sale, as is the case of over-the-counter retail sales. Mail order retailing meets this requirement, since the customer expects to have the product delivered at a future date. The results of a survey questionnaire directed to 400 manufacturers who are known to drop ship for mail order dealers will be evaluated. By narrowing the scope of the research to the mail order field, more exacting results can be obtained because all products are sold for future delivery, which is the exact condition required for drop shipping to function.

MANUFACTURERS WHO SELL THROUGH MAIL ORDER DEALERS

The manufacturer who sells products through mail order dealers has selected this channel of distribution for a number of reasons. Perhaps the product produced is a specialty item that has appeal other than price and is not ordinarily sold in retail stores, based on the very nature of the product. The product may have features such as mailability, high markup, market segmentation possibilities and numerous other factors which have appeared in the "checklists" of a good mail order product contained in various books on mail order. The manufacturer may also sell to wholesalers who sell to full-function retailers. However, if the manufacturer has limited funds for consumer advertising, the magazine or catalog promotions of a mail order retailer may increase the sales of the product for regular retailers with stock. A consumer may see the product in a mail order catalog and then purchase the item in a retail store.

If a manufacturer elects to market products through mail order dealers, the question may arise as to why they would not place their own mail order advertising in magazines and sell direct to the ultimate consumer. The manufacturer may produce only one product, and if they sold direct, the volume of business might not be as cost effective as selling through hundreds of mail order firms that would promote the product. Some manufacturers believe that lower marketing costs can be gained by eliminating middlemen, in spite of the fact that only about 4 percent of all goods are sold by U.S. manufacturers directly to retail consumers. All producers could sell direct to the public, however it is not necessarily less expensive to perform all of the functions of middlemen at the manufacturing level. The manufacturer may find it more profitable to drop ship products and shift the cost of consumer advertising to mail order dealers.

MAIL ORDER DEALERS: TO STOCK OR NOT TO STOCK

Selling by mail covers the gamut from some of the largest retailers to the smallest firms. Common among all mail order firms is the fact that catalogs, direct mail or advertising through other media are the prime means of selling to consumers for future delivery. Mail order firms have a number of common cost factors: overhead, inventory and advertising. If a mail order company stocks inventory, no one knows if adequate sales will result from mail order advertising. Ideally, inventory should equal sales. Manufacturers, in an effort to induce mail order firms to stock products, offer incentives in the form of quantity discounts. These incentives offered to mail order dealers may not be large enough to offset the costs and risks of holding inventory and possibly having unsalable merchandise.

Because the returns from mail order advertising are uncertain, the mail order dealer may seek manufacturers who will drop ship single-unit orders to their customers. Through drop shipping, the manufacturer becomes a stable source of supply that can furnish the exact amount of inventory at the time it is needed to fill orders. Although the inventory problems of mail order firms such as Sears Roebuck may not be critical, small mail order companies may balance the advantages of initiating drop ship orders against any pricing benefits gained by stocking inventory of the products sold. As an example, a mail order product may have a retail value of $40. The manufacturer may drop ship single units of the product to the customers of the dealer at 40 percent off the list price, or for $24. If the dealer stocks in quantities of one gross, the manufacturer may offer a discount of 50 percent off list. In this case, the dealer has the alternative of taking physical possession of inventory and performing a mailing function to customers, with the benefit of earning an additional 10 percent off the list price of the product. This extra 10 percent discount may not be worth the direct costs of stocking inventory, even if the manufacturer may "lend" the merchandise to the mail order dealer by the extension of net thirty days payment terms.

SAMPLE SELECTION

The hypothesis under consideration—drop shipping as a means for reducing marketing costs—was best studied by sending survey questionnaires to manufacturers who are known to drop ship products for mail order dealers. A survey directed to a purely random sample of all manufacturers would be impractical, as a large percentage of these firms would fail to respond to the survey if they do not provide drop shipping services. A list of 400 drop shipping manufacturers was used as the basis of the survey.

QUESTIONNAIRE DESIGN

The mail survey endeavored to determine the cost advantages and usage of drop shipping for the manufacturer and mail order dealer alike. The term *cost advantage* is taken in the broad sense to include various marketing functions, including financing, storage, inventory costs, advertising and other factors. Although the hypothesis studied assumes that there are cost advantages associated with drop shipping, every attempt was made to avoid leading questions in the survey. As mentioned, the cost advantages of drop shipping may be based on factors that include the marketing policies of both the drop shipper and mail order dealer alike. Substantiating that any one factor will reduce marketing costs is hampered to the extent that many companies do not know what their allocated marketing costs are in the first place.

Cost reduction implies that savings are made based on a change from an existing condition or that existing policies are less costly than an alternative method that could be used, however the effect of a change in one area may not be measurable in another.

The survey was directed to firms that drop ship for dealers. Because drop shipping is an existing condition, it is assumed that doing away with drop shipping and selling only to dealers that stock would be a more costly alternative. The other approach would be to study the marketing costs of firms that sell to dealers that stock inventory and attempt to show that drop shipping would reduce marketing costs. It is not the purpose of the survey to show that drop shipping a specific order will be less costly than selling to stocking middlemen. In a hypothetical case, it might be shown that drop shipments are more costly than selling to stocking dealers, yet it may be more costly to refuse to fill drop ship orders, if manufacturers might lose 50 percent of their dealers.

A problem in questionnaire design is based on the fact that lack of finances on the part of the manufacturer or dealer may be one reason to use drop shipping. A marketing policy is only as strong as its weakest link. In the example of the appliance display plan mentioned in chapter 1, it can hardly be said that the multimillion-dollar manufacturer of appliances that drop ships for dealers is financially weak. If there are indications of lack of funds for inventory, the retail appliance dealer more than likely has that problem. On the other hand, a manufacturer or stocking middleman may drop ship products for dealers because the firm may not be financially able to gain stocking dealers or extend credit and spend funds on consumer advertising. The mail order dealer likewise may prefer to advertise the products of a manufacturer, invest nothing in inventory, and use the drop shipping services of others. It would be difficult to ask the manufacturer the direct question: "Is lack of adequate financing, when considering inventory and promotion costs, the reason why your firm drop ships for dealers?" Few companies would admit to that fact. But manufacturers and dealers could refuse to deal in drop shipments if they had all the funds necessary to finance and stock all the required inventory.

THE SURVEY QUESTIONNAIRE

Following is a copy of the questionnaire directed to 400 manufacturers or prime stocking distributors that are known to drop ship products for mail order firms.

The analysis of the survey attempted to relate the results of the questionnaire to the hypothesis and to draw conclusions that will give insight into the function of drop shipping, particularly in reducing costs. The questionnaire mailed to 400 companies known to drop ship for mail order firms contained basic types of questions: factual yes-no answers, a ranking in order of preference, and opinion questions. Question 1 of the survey questionnaire was designed to determine whether the firm is a manufacturer or wholesaler, in addition to the type of merchandise sold and the price range. Question 2 determined the percentage of business done as drop shipments; questions 3 and 4 are ranking questions; question 5 the percentage of discounts; question 6 a ranking of answers; and 7 the option of doing away with drop shipping followed by question 8 on general opinions on the use of drop shipping.

RESULTS AND ANALYSIS

Of the 400 companies that were mailed the questionnaire, a total of 146 usable responses were received for a 36.5 percent return on the number of surveys sent. A few were returned with the answers to only one or two questions and were considered to be usable. Questions 3, 4 and 6 (ranking questions) often contained less than the total possible of ranking choices. As an example, the answer to question 3 may indicate only a 1 through 3 rank listing, rather than the full 1 through 6 ranking. If the respondent gave only the 1 through 3 ranking, the results were counted.

RETAIL PRICE RANGE AND TYPE OF PRODUCTS DROP SHIPPED

The results of the answers to question 1 indicated that of the 146 usable questionnaires, 128 of the firms were manufacturers or 87.6 percent of the total, and 18 companies or 12.4 percent were wholesalers that stocked merchandise. The products distributed included such items as belts, bakery supplies, books, novelties, wire products, looms, home appliances, stereo equipment, drugs, chemicals, housewares, optical goods, notions and many other types of products. Of the 146 firms, 66 percent sold goods with a retail value of between $1 and $10 in value; 21 percent between $10 and $25, and 13 percent sold products valued at over $25 (see table 1). The fact that 66 percent of the respondents sold products that had a retail price of $10 and below was based on the fact that few of the firms produced major appliances that would naturally have higher retail prices.

PERCENTAGE OF BUSINESS HANDLED AS DROP SHIPMENTS

Of the firms responding to question 2 (the percentage of business done as drop shipments), 24 percent of the firms did over 50 percent of their business as drop shipments. The breakdown for the remainder of the respondents is shown in table 2. It is assumed that the reciprocal of these percentages for each firm must represent merchandise sold to middlemen who stock inventory.

WHY MAIL ORDER DEALERS USE DROP SHIPPING SERVICES

The respondents to question 3 were requested to rank in the order of importance the reasons why they believed their dealers used the drop

CONFIDENTIAL DROP SHIPPING RESEARCH QUESTIONNAIRE

1. Are you a manufacturer? ( ) or a stocking wholesaler? ( ).
    Type of merchandise_____Retail price range
    $_____.

2. What percentage of your sales (estimated) are made to your
    mail order dealers as drop shipments? _____%

3. Please rank (1-6) in order if importance the reasons why
    you believe your mail order dealers use your drop shipping
    services.
    a. ( ) Dealers can spend more on promotion and advertising.
    b. ( ) Reduces the dealer's transportation costs.
    c. ( ) Lack of adequate capital.
    d. ( ) Cost advantages of drop shipping to the dealer
             are greater than the additional discounts they
             would earn if they stocked goods.
    e. ( ) Reduces order handling costs.
    f. ( ) Dealer spends nothing on inventory.
    g. ( ) Other reasons? _____.

4. Please rank (1-9) in order of importance the factors which
    guided your decision to drop ship for your mail order dealers.
    a. ( ) As a service to dealers.
    b. ( ) To reduce your order handling costs.
    c. ( ) The cost of selling to stocking wholesalers is
             too great.
    d. ( ) To shift mail order advertising costs to the
             dealer.
    e. ( ) Lack of funds for product promotion.
    f. ( ) To gain additional business.
    g. ( ) To reduce your own investment in production
             and inventory.

h. ( ) To gain mail order dealers as distributors.

i. ( ) Other reasons? _____.

5. What discounts off list prices do you offer on drop

    ship orders? _____%. Discounts if the dealer

    stocks merchandise? _____%. In what minimum

    quantity _____.

6. How was the difference in discounts on drop ship orders

    and orders shipped to stocking dealers determined?

    (Please rank, 1-4).

    a. ( ) Single unit drop shipments more costly,

              therefore lower discounts.

    b. ( ) Discounts designed to stimulate the dealer to

              stock goods.

    c. ( ) Lower costs of shipping in minimum quantities

              to stocking dealers.

    d. ( ) Other reasons? _____.

7. Would you prefer to do away with drop shipping entirely

and sell only to stocking mail order dealers? Yes ( ). No ( ).

8. On the reverse side of this sheet, please give your

    thoughts as to the greatest advantages and disadvantages

    of drop shipping from your standpoint and the standpoint

    of your dealers, particularly in the area of reducing

    costs.

                          *   *   *

shipping services of the manufacturer. Although all the answers to question 3 are possible reasons, the question was designed to determine the ones that were most important. Of the 136 respondents that answered this question, 70 firms (or 52 percent) ranked 3f. as the first choice (see table 3). The fact that the dealer spends nothing on inventory was the major reason why dealers used drop shipping. Answer 3f. was also selected by 46 firms (or 34 percent) of the respondents as the second choice. Answer 3c., lack of capital, was chosen as the second most important reason for a dealer's

TABLE 1

TABULATION OF RESPONSES TO SURVEY QUESTION 1

Retail dollar value of goods sold	Number of companies responding	Percentage
$1.00 - 2.00	29	20%
$2.00 - 10.00	68	46%
$10.00 - 25.00	30	21%
$25.00 and up	19	13%
Totals	146	100%

(Source material for all tables, returned questionnaires)

TABLE 2

TABULATION OF RESPONSES TO SURVEY QUESTION 2

Percentage of business	Number of companies responding	Percentage
1 - 5%	30	22%
5 - 10%	20	15%
10 - 25%	22	17%
25 - 50%	15	22%
50 - 100%	32	24%
Totals	119	100%

use of drop shipping as indicated by 35 percent of the respondents. The relationship between these factors is evident, since a dealer who may lack capital cannot spend it on inventory. These factors relate to the hypothesis in that the function of warehouse or storage costs are eliminated since the inventory is not stocked by the middlemen. In addition, capital itself is a cost factor, since money tied up in inventory represents an investment that can be recovered only after the products are sold. The exact cost reductions would vary from one company to another. Answer 3e. regarding the re-

TABLE 3

TABULATION OF RESPONSES TO SURVEY QUESTION 3

Survey question	Number of respondents answering questions, ranked in order of preference					
	1st	2nd	3rd	4th	5th	6th
3 a.	6	10	24	10	30	26
3 b.	8	6	22	28	28	20
3 c.	48	24	22	10	6	18
3 d.	4	18	22	20	12	16
3 e.	0	32	28	26	14	12
3 f.	70	46	10	4	12	0
Totals	136	136	128	108	102	92

duction of order handling costs was the third greatest reason for using drop shipping, according to the survey results. The reduction of order handling costs was selected by 32 firms (or 24 percent) as a second choice, and 28 firms selected 3e. as a third choice. The answers do not reveal how much the order handling costs are reduced on drop shipments, as compared to order handling on sales made to stocking dealers. The terms costs and cost reduction are relative terms, and few mail order dealers would be able to determine exact cost savings through the elimination of storage, order handling and the investment in inventory.

WHY MANUFACTURERS DROP SHIP FOR MAIL ORDER DEALERS

There are numerous reasons why a manufacturer or stocking wholesaler drop ships for middlemen, and each of the answers in question 4 may not apply to every company surveyed. Question 4 showed a definite trend toward answer 4f. as the reason why manufacturers drop ship for dealers. To gain additional business was given by 48 percent of the 142 respondents to this question as the reason why they drop ship (see table 4). Answer 4h., regarding the gaining of mail order dealers, was the second most important reason given by 42 percent of the respondents as to why manufacturers drop ship. Answer 4a., the service factor related to drop shipping, had the third largest number of first choices or 15 percent of the

TABLE 4

TABULATION OF RESPONSES TO SURVEY QUESTION 4

Survey question	Number of respondents answering questions, ranked in order of preference							
	1st	2nd	3rd	4th	5th	6th	7th	8th
4 a.	22	20	36	20	12	8	2	2
4 b.	4	2	6	16	18	20	8	8
4 c.	2	0	8	12	20	10	12	10
4 d.	6	16	10	14	8	14	10	4
4 e.	8	6	4	6	10	8	16	12
4 f.	68	26	20	8	2	2	4	6
4 g.	2	4	4	10	6	10	16	22
4 h.	28	54	20	8	8	6	2	2
Totals	142	128	108	94	84	78	70	66

respondents, in addition to 15 percent of the second choices. Although answers 4f. and 4h. have similar meanings, they differ in that drop shipping services could be offered to increase sales to existing dealers that usually stock merchandise. To gain mail order dealers indicates that the manufacturer may offer drop shipping services to acquire new dealers they would not have gained unless drop shipping services were offered as an inducement to do business.

DISCOUNTS ON DROP SHIPMENTS VERSUS SALES TO STOCKING DEALERS

The results of survey question 5 in table 5 indicate that manufacturers and stocking wholesalers offered the following discounts off list prices of products sold on a drop shipped basis as follows: 60 percent of the respondents offered a 40 percent discount; 29 percent offered a 50 percent discount; 4 percent offered a 50 and 10 percent (list, less 50 percent, less 10 percent) discount; and only 2 percent offered over a 60 percent discount. The respondents also indicated the following discounts off list prices on sales made to stocking dealers: 20 percent offered a 40 percent discount; 29 percent offered a 50 percent discount; 43 percent offered a 50 and 10 percent (list, less 50 percent, less 10 percent) discount; and 8 percent

TABLE 5

TABULATION OF RESPONSES TO SURVEY QUESTION 5

	Percentage discount off list prices offered by number of responding companies			
	40%	50%	50-10%	60% and up
Discounts on drop shipments	90	40	6	2
Discounts offered to stocking dealers	26	38	56	10
Totals	116	78	62	12

offered over a 60 percent discount. The minimum quantities purchased by stocking dealers, based on survey results, varied to such an extent that tabulation of this factor was not possible. A number of firms indicated that they offered a 50 percent discount off list prices on merchandise on sales to stocking dealers, but did not mention the minimum quantity that would be shipped at that discount. The quantities noted on other survey responses varied from one unit to a gross or more. Of major significance is the fact that there was a 10 to 20 percent difference between the discount offered on sales to stocking dealers and on drop shipped orders. The respondents indicated that a 40 percent discount was offered by the largest number of firms supplying products on a single-unit drop ship basis. Some companies offered the same discount on drop shipped orders and orders from stocking dealers, but the majority of firms offered a discount differential.

Some of the discounts overlapped in that one manufacturer offered a 40 percent discount on drop shipped orders and 50 percent discount to stocking dealers. Other firms allowed a 50 percent discount on drop shipped orders and a 50 and 10 percent discount or more if the dealer stocked the goods. A discount differential of 10 to 20 percent was the usual case when comparing drop shipped orders and those sold to stocking dealers. The difference in discounts could be used to stimulate dealers to stock or to cover any extra costs that may be incurred by the manufacturer in providing drop shipping services.

DIFFERENCE IN DISCOUNTS ON DROP SHIPPED ORDERS AND ORDERS SOLD TO STOCKING MIDDLEMEN

Of the survey respondents, 58 percent answered question 6a. as a first choice (see table 6). This indicates that single-unit drop shipments are

TABLE 6

TABULATION OF RESPONSES TO SURVEY QUESTION 6

Survey question	Number of respondents answering questions, ranked in order of preference		
	1st	2nd	3rd
6.a	58	20	18
6 b.	32	32	20
6 c.	10	36	40
Totals	100	88	78

more costly to handle, therefore the discounts are not as great as if the dealers stocked the products. Although this appears to refute the hypothesis, one factor to consider is transportation costs. Many of the respondents stated that single-unit drop shipped orders are delivered to the customers of the dealer at the cost of the drop shipper. Orders sold to stocking dealers were shipped f.o.b. by the manufacturer. In the case of f.o.b. shipments, the dealer that stocks the merchandise obviously pays for the cost of shipping. Since most drop shipments are delivered at the expense of the manufacturer, this factor could narrow the margin between the two discounts. One reason why the discounts may be lower on drop shipped orders is to cover the costs of "in the mail" delivery which are often paid for the drop shipper. The absorption of shipping costs by the drop shipper may also be based on an effort to reduce paperwork and billing. Because many drop shipped transactions are "cash with order," the dealer sends the drop shipper the net amount after deducting 40 to 50 percent off the list price, which would include shipping costs to the customer. The manufacturer may not know the exact shipping cost which would be covered by the smaller-than-usual discount on drop shipments, or the drop shipper could offer functional discounts and add a fixed charge for handling each drop shipped order, rather than billing for the exact shipping costs.

Although sales made to stocking dealers are usually sold on open account, the f.o.b. delivery charge can be billed to the dealer, along with the cost of the goods. It might be difficult to receive a cash-with-order drop ship order and then bill the dealer for the postage or delivery charges. The answers to question 5 indicated that there usually is a 10 to 20 percent differential between the discount on drop shipped orders and sales made to dealers that stock. It is logical that manufacturers want dealers to stock merchandise, however the incentive to stock in quantity on the part of the dealer to some extent is based on the larger discounts gained by stocking merchandise, in spite of the fact that there are many costs and risks associated with carrying inventory.

MANUFACTURERS WHO WOULD PREFER TO DO AWAY WITH DROP SHIPPING

Of the firms responding to question 7 as to whether they would prefer to do away with drop shipping entirely, 36 percent of the firms stated that they would prefer to stop providing drop shipping services, however 50 percent of these companies sold products that retailed for less than $2. In addition, of the firms that would prefer to do away with drop shipping, 67 percent indicated that less than 5 percent of their business was handled as drop shipments. Lack of interest in providing drop shipping services on the part of drop shippers is no doubt based on low retail prices of the product and small volume of drop ship business.

ADVANTAGES AND DISADVANTAGES OF DROP SHIPPING

Of the firms that answered the questionnaire, 50 percent gave written opinions as to the usage of drop shipping. These responses ranged from single comments to full typewritten pages. A few of the quotations from the survey are as follows:

> Advantages of drop shipping: To manufacturer or wholesaler: To obtain additional business which would not otherwise be obtained from small dealers who do not have capital or facilities to stock. Also, drop ship orders are "cash with order basis" which enables us to sell to otherwise undesirable credit risks. To dealer: No warehousing required. No inventory, no packing facilities, no purchases until order is received and paid for by the end user. Business is purely and simply an advertising and bookkeeping function with 100% drop ship.

Another respondent stated:

> As a dealer, drop shipping is the only way which allows him to get into business on a shoestring. Investment requirements are at a minimum and no stock is required. If the dealer finds that the product is not moving too well, or he no longer is interested in selling it, he has no inventory to worry about, no stock to dispose of in an emergency, and no money tied up in merchandise. Possible disadvantage—delay in filling orders.

Another respondent commented: "The greatest advantage to this style of merchandising is the simple fact that the manufacturer and dealer alike can both use the same inventory. It is obvious that this is a more efficient method if all cooperate as they should." Another respondent: "Greatest advantage to me is it attracts business from many small operators, and I do not have to spend money on advertising." While another states: "Drop shipping is excellent business for a newly patented product. Drop shipping keeps costs down for both the manufacturer and mail order house. This is important when production and sales are small. Both need to meet higher costs which will go down when volume of sales increases. In this way, the retail price is kept realistic and unchanged from the beginning. I will keep drop shipping facilities available."

Another respondent states: "We drop ship for one of the large auto manufacturers to their wholesalers. By offering to drop ship we hold the business. For the customer this means no warehouse space tied up, plus no inventory investment. We pointed out these advantages to the consumer in our selling program." Yet another respondent: "Main advantage is wider advertising at minimum cost to us and immediate payment before goods are shipped." Another stated: "Eliminates difficult situations with dealers who optimistically or ignorantly order large wholesale shipments, then find pretext to want to return most of them. Eliminates credit problems (cash basis for drop ship)." Another states: "Little credit problems—most drop shipments are payment with order. Sales activity by a number of customers produces a small but steady flow of orders which helps regulate stock level and diminishes overload of inventory.

Another respondent indicates: "Primarily this method of selling is an inducement to obtain dealer support in testing the sales appeal for a product. This is a two-way street in that once the dealer is convinced a product will sell enough to warrant his stocking an adequate inventory to fill order promptly, he will maintain stocks of merchandise in such volume that it will match his anticipated sales and his capital requirements." Another responded: "Credit problems have been eliminated to zero, shipments are made on all orders within 24 hours of receipt." Another stated: "From our standpoint, drop shipping in quantity is profitable since we eliminate advertising costs completely. We do prefer, however, stocking dealer arrangements since this usually generated higher volume, probably because dealers are considerably larger and do much greater volume of business."

Another manufacturer states: "From our point of view, there is no disadvantage. By drop shipping for many new accounts that come to us, we are able to increase our total sales, so that's an advantage for us." Another respondent wrote at length:

Drop shipping is used quite extensively by both small and large mail order firms, and this method of operation, I am sure, has enabled several indi-

viduals to start in a mail order business in a small way and gradually build
a successful mail order business. I personally know of one man who started
selling by using wholesale discount catalogs and having all merchandise
drop shipped. Within about three years his business had grown so rapidly
that he had started stocking his own merchandise and was occupying a
two-story building. I personally have sold several hundred thousand dollars
worth of merchandise through the drop ship method. All I did was distribute
catalogs and sales literature and when orders arrived, I would send them
on to the wholesaler, jobber or factory to be drop shipped direct to my
customers. The entire operation was carried out on a strict cash basis. I
would deduct my profit, and then send the balance on to the drop shipper.

ANALYSIS OF DROP SHIPPING SURVEY RESULTS

The results of the survey indicated some basic factors concerning drop
shipping as a marketing function. There appears to be a lower limit to the
retail value of products that can profitably be drop shipped in single units.
As mentioned, 50 percent of the firms that would prefer to do away with
drop shipping handled products with a retail value of less than $10, however
this same group did less than 5 percent of their sales volume as drop
shipments.

The survey revealed that because the mail order dealer spends nothing
on inventory, that was the greatest reason for their use of drop shipping,
followed by the apparent lack of capital to finance inventory. The hypothesis under study relates to the use of drop shipping as a means of reducing
costs. Although the direct costs of capital and inventory would vary from
one dealer to another, it is obvious that there is a link between lack of
capital and the elimination of inventory costs. Either capital, which would
ordinarily be spent on inventory, is freed for other purposes, or the cost
of borrowing is eliminated.

Cost reduction factors related to drop shipping may include storage,
financing, transportation, advertising, order handling and other expenses
that may vary from one firm to another. The dealer who has no investment
in inventory through drop shipping incurs no storage costs, which are a
fixed expense, regardless of how much inventory is kept on hand. Any
cost savings resulting from drop shipping must be balanced against the
possible advantage of additional functional or quantity discounts that are
usually offered stocking dealers.

The survey results indicated that getting additional business was one of
the main reasons why a manufacturer is willing to drop ship orders for
dealers, and cost reduction factors were a third choice. The bulk of the
advertising and marketing costs are shifted to the mail order dealer, while
the manufacturer can maintain a centralized inventory which is drawn upon
by many dealers. This factor may reduce the initial inventory investment

costs of the manufacturer, since there is no need to "lend" inventory to stocking dealers for thirty days, with the hope that payment will be forthcoming.

A mail order dealer who stocks merchandise usually orders in quantities that can be sold within or close to the thirty-day net payment term period and have a reorder point to keep a continual flow of outgoing orders and incoming inventory. The stocking dealer anticipates enough sales to cover at least a portion of inventory costs within the thirty days when net billing is due. The alternative may be a decision to take an additional 2 percent discount for payment within ten days, if these terms are offered by the supplier. But again the question arises as to the comparative costs of the loss of the 2 percent discount versus the "free" use of the inventory for twenty extra days without payment. There is a similarity to an extent between the purchase of inventory on open account by a dealer and the use of drop shipping services of the manufacturer. In each case the dealer has the use of the inventory of the manufacturer without immediate cost if thirty-day net terms are offered by the source of supply.

Advertising costs could also be studied on the basis of survey results, in that most of the consumer promotion costs are incurred by the mail order dealer in the form of catalogs or other types of direct response advertising. The manufacturer has the cost of gaining dealers, whether they stock or use drop shipping services. The survey results indicated that one of the main reasons for offering drop shipping services by the manufacturer was to gain additional dealers. On this basis it is assumed that if by offering drop shipping services, the manufacturer can acquire more dealers, which can only add to sales volume, reduce costs and add to profits.

On a broad economic scope, total transportation costs may be reduced through drop shipping. As an example, a mail order dealer in California may receive an order from a customer in New Jersey. The order is sent to the drop shipper, a manufacturer located in New York, who fills the order. The shipping costs from New York to New Jersey would be paid for by either the dealer or manufacturer, depending on their arrangement. But if the dealer in California stocked inventory, the merchandise would first have to be shipped from New York all the way to California, repacked and reshipped to the customer of the dealer in New Jersey. If the dealer stocked the product, it would be shipped some 6,000 miles back and forth across the country, while the drop shipment might move the product less than a hundred miles.

In summary, the survey results offer some conclusions regarding cost reduction factors of drop shipping.

For the manufacturer or drop shipper:

1. Lower total costs by gaining additional dealers
2. Smaller initial inventory requirements, since both the manufacturer and many dealers draw upon the same centralized inventory

3. Elimination of billing and credit problems on cash-with-order business
4. Greater profits by extending smaller-than-usual discounts on drop shipped orders

For the mail order dealer:

1. Elimination of the cost of capital needed to stock inventory
2. Reduction or elimination of warehousing, storage, packing and overhead costs
3. Allowing the use of capital to be spent on advertising and marketing

REASONS FOR DROP SHIPPING, RANKED BY IMPORTANCE

All of the choices noted on the questionnaire may reduce costs through drop shipping. The choices ranked by importance still do not give a clear-cut dollar amount of savings that can be directly related to drop shipping. A cost accountant would be required to determine all the cost factors related to drop shipments and to sales made to dealers that stock inventory and then to compare the total cost differential. The survey is directed to ranking descriptions of marketing functions that all have a relationship to cost reduction but may have different levels of importance to various companies. The dollar value of the difference between discounts offered on drop shipments and the discounts offered on orders that are stocked by dealers does not necessarily measure the total cost saving differential between the two.

It would be difficult to develop a questionnaire that would show actual dollar cost savings of drop shipping as compared to sales made to stocking dealers. Most firms can't isolate every marketing cost and are therefore unable to compare alternate marketing methods. A study of the policy formation function of companies may indicate the economic benefits of drop shipping as related to capital budgeting, finance, credit extension, warehousing, transportation and advertising.

4

Functions and Services of Drop Shippers

FACTORS AFFECTING POLICIES OF DROP SHIPPERS

Any firm that provides drop shipping services is confronted with a number of decisions: determining the minimum quantity to be drop shipped, handling requests for samples, special packaging for drop shipped orders, storage of inventory, order processing, order handling, billing and shipping in addition to contracts with dealers and policies regarding dealer aids, photos, catalogs, syndications and other aspects. These and other policy decisions all have a relationship to the cost effectiveness and profitability of providing drop shipping services.

Not all manufacturers or other stocking entities are willing to provide drop shipping services for middlemen. The unwillingness to drop ship single units of a product often concerns the very nature of the merchandise. If a product could not realistically be sold by mail at a retail price of over $3, and if by chance the product weighs 10 ounces, the possibility of any profit on such a sale may be diminished to the point that the stocking source would not provide drop shipping services in single units under any circumstances, regardless of who pays for the shipping costs. The fact that a product has a relatively low retail price along with high shipping costs may preclude the item from being a product that could be drop shipped, but it could also preclude the item from consideration as a mail order product in the first place. The item would probably not be a profitable single-unit mail order product even if the middleman stocked the product in quantity. Very low priced items seldom are profitable for direct response promotion for future delivery—no matter who ships it.

Any marketing policy should be based on the objective to maximize profits, and if drop shipping cannot contribute to the profit of a manufacturer, it is doubtful that the service would be offered to middlemen. The decision to offer drop shipping services can be affected by the retail price of the product, the resulting wholesale price and shipping costs along with overhead. The cost of order processing, order handling and shipping are relatively fixed for any firm whether it is the manufacturer performing drop shipping services or a mail order firm handling single-unit orders. It would probably cost the same amount for a manufacturer to pack and ship a $50 necklace or an item that may have a retail price of only $3. Every product has a margin of profit or volume of business that will allow drop shipping to function to the satisfaction of the manufacturer or stocking entity and, in turn, the middleman.

Although profit is the guiding light in the formulation of any marketing policy of a manufacturer, other factors may or may not affect the decision to drop ship products for middlemen. A few manufacturers will only drop ship in an emergency and not as a regular course of business. The supply source may not offer any indication that they will provide drop shipping services in product or wholesale literature. Manufacturers on occasion may drop ship single units as a special favor to selected dealers. Other firms may state that they never deal in drop shipments, when in reality they may have unwritten arrangements with dealers who request certain orders to be drop shipped.

Some governmental regulations, however, concern the relationship between the manufacturer and the middleman. The Robinson-Patman Act covers this relationship in particular with the general connotation that all of the customers of the manufacturer must be treated on an equal basis. Although the performance of drop shipping by a manufacturer is a voluntary service, it is possible that once the service is offered, the arrangement may fall under Sec. 2(e) of the Act, which makes it unlawful to discriminate in favor of one purchaser against another purchaser of a product bought for resale or offering terms not accorded to all purchasers equally. This section is very similar to another portion of the Robinson-Patman Act that the offer or extension of advertising allowances to retailers by a manufacturer must also be offered to all other retailers on an equal or proportional basis. If a drop shipper provides free photos, graphics, catalog sheets, color separations or other advertising aids or allowances to one dealer or distributor, then the same material must be offered to all others. All of these provisions can be distilled to the premise that a manufacturer should treat all dealers on an equal basis, and if drop shipping services are provided for one mail order firm, then the drop shipper should provide similar services to all other mail order firms.

The marketing policies of a manufacturer must be reviewed in light of existing laws and the interpretation of the law, particularly those that fall under the domain of the Federal Trade Commission (FTC). Because the FTC makes rulings on a case-by-case basis, it is difficult to gain definitive guidelines. Therefore, the price of the products and projected profits, along with governmental regulations, should be reviewed when marketing policies are established on drop shipping. The marketing managers of many manufacturers are often unresponsive to the needs of middlemen, mail order firms and other retailers. Often marketing policies are developed on the basis of a tradition or "custom of the trade."

Drop shipping services are often offered to mail order firms by small manufacturers, particularly since some of the retail advertising costs are shifted to direct response marketers. If by offering drop shipping services manufacturers can get their products listed in the mail order catalogs of several hundred direct marketers, so much the better. Every advertising exposure in print media that is paid for by the middleman has given the manufacturer product promotion that might be unavailable through any other method. Manufacturers who do not offer drop shipping services may reduce the potential number of dealers or mail order firms that are willing to promote the product.

MINIMUM QUANTITIES OF PRODUCTS DROP SHIPPED BY STOCKING ENTITIES

It is almost mandatory that a drop shipper handle single units for retail mail order firms. The customers of the mail order dealer who sells at retail will in all probability order a single unit of the product, and all aspects of filling orders have to be geared to single-unit order processing. Obviously, if two or more units of the same product are to be drop shipped to the same customer, the total number could be combined in the same shipping container. Drop shippers who service wholesalers or industrial distributors may require a minimum drop shipped order such as one dozen, six dozen, a gross or more. A manufacturer may package the product in a mailable corrugated carton containing twelve units, and this factory-sealed carton may be the minimum quantity acceptable as a drop shipped order. A wholesaler could establish the minimum quantity order that would be accepted from a retailer that would coincide with the minimum quantity order that would be drop shipped by the manufacturer or stocking entity. Each manufacturer would have to determine the minimum quantity they would be willing to drop ship, depending on the "standard quantity" pack, value of the product, shipping costs and other factors.

PRICING POLICIES ON DROP SHIPPED PRODUCTS

Manufacturers or middlemen who stock merchandise and provide drop shipping services for dealers or distributors have no doubt determined that a profit can be made on such orders, based on the single-unit drop shipped prices that have been established on the products sold. Although the FTC frowns on the printing of a so-called retail price on literature identified as being that of the manufacturer, the wholesale prices of drop shipped products have to be determined. The manufacturer has to start somewhere in order to find a profitable single-unit drop ship price on products offered to dealers or distributors.

As an example, if we assume that the cost of materials, labor, overhead, storage and other fixed and variable costs can be determined, and if a markup or profit margin is applied to these costs, we might find that a $5, in-the-mail single-unit drop ship price for a product would be profitable, with a suggested retail price of $10 or higher. However, based on a few FTC rulings, some manufacturers have been brought to task for placing a retail price or even a "suggested" retail price on a product package, since it is the contention of the FTC that the product may never have been intended to sell at the printed retail or suggested retail price indicated on the package. The former practice of having a list price of $10 for a product established by the manufacturer and then applying a 50 percent discount from the list price to create a $5 single-unit drop shipped price has given way to the formulation of the drop ship price of $5 based on cost, with the retail price left to the pressures of the free enterprise system.

Before the Fair Trade laws were abolished, a manufacturer could not only indicate a suggested retail price for products, but establish the actual retail price at which retailers within a state were required to sell the products. These laws were supposedly maintained to protect small retailers and mail order companies that could not compete with large mass retailers. The mass merchandisers also sold Fair Traded products at the same prices as small retailers, however the large stores were able to maintain dominance in the marketplace with their locations, size and efficiency. The large retailers and mail order firms had the advantage of quantity discounts that could add as much as 10 percent and 15 percent to gross margins.

The legality of the establishment of fixed retail prices on products also allowed manufacturers to produce vast amounts of point-of-purchase and co-op advertising in which the retail price of the product was included. From the standpoint of mail order firms, the manufacturer could legally supply camera-ready artwork for various sized advertisements for mail order catalogs with the retail price clearly stated. In addition, manufacturers could supply preprinted minicatalogs and circulars available with the name and address of the retailer or mail order firm that indicated the suggested or fixed retail prices on all products. When the Fair Trade laws were repealed, the general rule was now interpreted to disallow manufacturers from indicating or establishing a retail price for products. They could no longer require a mail order firm or other retailer to sell their products at a list or suggested retail price. However, the practice of using suggested retail prices on hang tags and packaging still exists, although manufacturers cannot enforce adherence to the suggested retail price, which may or may not be realistic. Many manufacturers indicate a suggested retail price for their products in wholesale literature upon which functional discounts to middlemen are computed.

Most consumer groups, including those sponsored by local governments, have various rules designed for the protection of consumers. In certain cities, the suggested retail price printed on the package or hang tag is supposedly no longer allowed. The theory behind the elimination of the suggested retail price is to stimulate competition and to protect the retail buying public from unrealistic prices. This policy works well for consumer groups when it serves their interests. The case in point concerns retailers and mail order firms that offer products above the suggested retail price indicated by the manufacturer. In such an instance, the consumer protection groups do a turnaround in their policy by requiring the posting of the suggested retail price. But if the establishment of the suggested retail price by the manufacturer is illegal, how can a mail order firm know what this price should be or if the firm is charging prices higher than an illegally set or phantom price set by the manufacturer? A manufacturer may have indicated to a mail order firm that an item has a suggested retail price of $10, however the mail order marketer cannot state that fact to the consumer unless the retailer charges a price that is higher than the $10 suggested retail price indicated by the manufacturer.

There are perhaps a good many arguments in favor of a suggested retail price established by the manufacturer. Whether the price is realistic or not, a suggested retail price established by a manufacturer is no more difficult to cope with by a consumer than if a mail order firm arbitrarily places a price on a product on a take-it-or-leave-it basis—without any reference to a suggested retail price. While the old Fair Trade laws that required every mail order firm or retailer in the state to sell a product at a price fixed by the manufacturer may have reduced competition, the use of a suggested retail price has value, even though these prices are often discounted.

The suggested retail price gives the consumer a guideline on which to make a buying decision. As an example, a loaf of bread may be prepriced by the baker at 98 cents. The consumer, knowing that the item has been prepriced, will pay the same amount in a large grocery chain store or in an all-night delicatessen that might be tempted to charge $1.25 or $1.50 for the same loaf of bread. The placing of a suggested retail price on a product package by the manufacturer puts an obvious lid on the price that would normally be charged by a retailer.

In the past, the use of a suggested retail or list price on a product formed the basis for the discount, discount price and the discount retailer. If there were no suggested retail prices in the first place, upon what price would the discount to the ultimate consumer be based? If suggested retail prices indicated by the manufacturer were eliminated, then a discount to the customer would have to be based on an arbitrary price established by the mail order firm or retailer, even though there was no serious intent to sell the product at that higher price. The same circumstances occur when a manufacturer sets an artificially high suggested retail price, and retailers can then apply discounts of their own choosing.

Suggested retail prices established by manufacturers also form the basis for functional and chain discounts. If the suggested retail price established by the manufacturer is $10 per unit, various discounts off that price can form wholesale or distributor prices, based on various quantities, such as less 40 percent, less 40 percent and 10 percent, less 50 percent, less 50 percent and 10 percent, and so on. This system of determining wholesale prices is still widely used, even though the manufacturer has little power to insure that the retailer or middleman will sell the products at the suggested price.

PRICING POLICIES ON PRODUCT SAMPLES SOLD TO MIDDLEMEN

Regardless of how the in-the-mail wholesale price on single-unit drop shipments is determined, the supplier of drop shipping services must decide whether to charge the same single-unit drop ship price when a dealer orders a single unit "sample" of merchandise or whether to charge the suggested retail price or some other price between the two. There are several pros and cons for each pricing policy.

The manufacturer or stocking entity has determined that the price charged on a single-unit drop shipment will allow a profit. This fact is obvious to a mail order dealer or distributor since the stocking entity has agreed to drop ship at that wholesale price, and the stocking entity would hardly sell merchandise at a loss. If the stocking entity requires that samples of merchandise are purchased at the retail or suggested retail price, the dealer may feel that the supplier is in effect a retailer, since retail prices are being charged for single-unit samples. If the stocking source requires that samples be purchased at any cost that is higher than the single-unit drop ship price, the dealer can always issue a drop ship order at the net wholesale price and have the merchandise shipped to a friend or relative. In this way the stocking source of supply has no way of determining if the order is a legitimate drop shipment or one for a merchandise sample. The implication lies in the possibility that the dealer may order a single unit of merchandise at the wholesale price for the personal use of the dealer, without any serious intent of promoting the product for resale.

The other aspect of offering samples of merchandise at a single-unit drop ship price concerns the fact that the stocking entity may be more interested in selling single-unit samples than supplying merchandise for resale through drop shipping. In this case, the wholesale single-unit price in effect becomes the retail price as far as the stocking entity is concerned. From the standpoint of the mail order dealer or distributor, much can be learned by careful examination of the sales literature of the manufacturer. In seeking product sources for resale through drop shipping, it would not be worthwhile for a dealer to use a product source that may be soliciting retail sales at wholesale drop shipped prices.

One indication in determining the motives of the drop shipping source concerns the means and methods of gaining dealers. If a manufacturer or stocking entity advertises in consumer magazines and offers a catalog of items at wholesale prices in single units—without any real concern as to whether the firm ordering the merchandise is really interested in selling the products through drop shipping or stocking—the merchandise supplier in this case may be performing the function of a retailer, regardless of whether the wholesale prices of the merchandise are realistic or not.

The basic assumption on the part of both the supplier and user of drop shipping services should be one of good faith. The supplier of services should be interested in gaining distributors and offering prompt drop ship order fulfillment. The dealers who use the drop shipping services of a manufacturer have to assume that the wholesale prices are realistic and should agree to conform with the terms and conditions of sale. Samples of merchandise offered by the stocking entity should be available to dealers at a net single-unit drop shipped price. Any other price would raise the issue that the stocking entity is attempting to charge an extra amount for samples or use the higher price as a qualification for becoming a dealer. The stocking entity must assume that the motive of the dealer in ordering a sample of merchandise is for use in product evaluation, examination and resale.

PACKAGING FOR SINGLE-UNIT DROP SHIPMENTS

The manufacturer or stocking entity that offers single-unit drop shipping services must package products in containers that can protect the merchandise and that can be shipped via third-class mail, parcel post, United Parcel Service (UPS) or freight, depending on the size and weight of the container. Numerous types of mailing boxes and cartons can meet the exact dimensions of the product, including packing materials. Trade magazines of the packaging or container industry can offer names of suppliers. The drop shipper should anticipate what portion of total inventory should be kept on hand in prepackaged individual mailers, based on expected sales volume of single-unit drop shipments from all sources. The order filling process is usually simple, in that the dealer will supply a preaddressed shipping label to be attached to the carton. The cartons might be stored partially sealed, in the event that a dealer may want to have a packing slip or literature enclosed in the carton. However, there should be a clear agreement as to what type of literature the manufacturer can include in the package, which is usually restricted to directions for use or assembly of the product and guarantee or warranty cards. Packing materials usually are used to protect loose merchandise or products packaged in light-weight containers, often printed in full color, which were originally designed for retail store display, but not suitable for use as shipping containers.

FACTORY-SEALED CORRUGATED CARTONS

In years past, over-the-counter merchandise sold by department stores or specialty shops was usually removed from all packaging material supplied by the manufacturer and placed on the shelf or counter for display and sale. After being sold, the product was then wrapped and placed in a bag or other packaging supplied by the retail store. As self-service in stores became more prominent and centralized checkout counters replaced the declining number of retail clerks, the impact on the type of packaging provided by the manufacturer became more evident. In addition to sturdy, store display packaging, often in full color, many products were appearing on store shelves in individual 200-pound test, sealed corrugated cartons. These products included many types of small appliances, consumer electronics, housewares and sporting goods in addition to big ticket items such as TV sets, refrigerators and room air conditioners.

There are a number of reasons for a trend toward corrugated carton packaging. Perhaps the most obvious is the fact that damage in transit can be greatly reduced when individual units of a product are sealed in corrugated cartons. The cost savings based on a small number of broken or damaged items many offset the additional cost of the carton and any increase in shipping costs based on the total weight of the container. Insurance charges, based on the freight classification of the inner pack corrugated cartons, may be at a lower rate than if the merchandise was bulk packed, nested or separated by partitions, tissue paper or other packaging materials.

Factory-sealed corrugated cartons are also used by the manufacturer when the product may require assembly by the purchaser. The parts to the product may be packed in plastic bags or envelopes, along with the directions for assembly and use. The sealed carton assures the consumer that all the nuts, bolts, parts and instructions are intact within the box. Likewise, in the case of small appliances, all the accessories can be sealed within the individual carton.

The impact of the factory-sealed carton on the psychology of the retail consumer has also been a factor. A customer may hesitate to purchase a product that has been on a shelf unboxed. It may have become shopworn, damaged or used as a demonstrator. The item may also have become separated from the parts, accessories and directions for use. If the product is sold on the basis of a warranty supplied by the manufacturer, the warranty statement and owner registration card may have become misplaced or lost. Unpackaged products displayed on the shelf are often sold at great marked down prices. They are usually classified as floor models, demonstrators or samples. The fact that such merchandise is sold at reduced prices indicates that depreciation begins rapidly once the product is removed from the carton or packaging supplied by the manufacturer.

The growth of the catalog showroom as a type of retailer has added to the use of the factory-sealed corrugated carton. It is understood by the consumer that merchandise selection will be made by examining a floor model or sample in the display area of the showroom and that the product will be received by the public at the pickup counter. In certain product classifications, the buying public not only expects to receive a factory-sealed corrugated carton but demands such packaging to assure that new, factory fresh merchandise is being received.

Why is the factory-sealed corrugated carton relevant to drop shipping? If a product is packaged in a factory-sealed carton, and it can be identified by the name and model number of the manufacturer, the retail consumer has a better means of comparison shopping on the basis of price. The level of confidence in the eyes of the consumer is enhanced when the sealed corrugated carton of merchandise is uniform throughout all channels of distribution. If a consumer orders a product by mail in a factory-sealed carton, identified by the stock number of the manufacturer, the consumer is assured that the merchandise shipped is exactly the same as it is sold in a retail store. Many of the factory-sealed cartons are so designed that the product can be shipped via the post office and UPS without an outer carton. However, since many appliances and consumer electronics are high pilferage items, an additional, slightly oversized carton may be used as the shipping container. The double boxing of such merchandise gives additional protection to the merchandise and hides the identity of the merchandise while in transit. The factory-sealed corrugated shipping carton can aid direct response marketers in that mail order consumers can order by the stock number of the manufacturer.

SHIPPING COSTS AND METHODS ON DROP SHIPMENTS

A wide variety of products are offered by manufacturers and distributors on a drop ship basis. These products range in weight from several ounces to industrial machinery that may weigh a ton. However, most consumer products can be drop shipped via third-class mail, parcel post, UPS or motor freight. On packages up to 4 ounces in weight, there is no difference in the single-unit, third-class and first-class U.S. Postal Service rates. Packages up to 15.9 ounces can qualify for commercial third-class mail rates, however a yearly mailing permit is required, and to qualify for these reduced rates, there must be a minimum of 200 pieces or 50 pounds shipped at one time. At the commercial third-class rate, up to 3.36 ounces can be shipped for only 16.7 cents, and this relatively low rate can have an impact on the costs of volume shippers of merchandise.

A manufacturer performing drop shipping services may have to wait until there are enough accumulated orders to reach the minimum requirements for commercial third-class rates, and this factor may delay shipments. If a drop shipper has a large number of dealers creating a constant flow of single-unit orders, the drop shipper has a better chance of meeting the minimum quantities or weight than a small mail order dealer who may only receive ten to twenty orders a day. There is a high incentive to accumulate orders to reach the 200 piece or 50 pound minimums on the part of the drop shipper or dealer who stocks merchandise and fills orders.

The profit margin on drop shipped products that are relatively low in price may be affected by mailing rates. As an example, the single piece third-class rate for 8.5 ounces is $1.20, while the commercial bulk rate for the same weight is 32.1 cents. The difference of 88 cents for each unit may represent a good portion of the profit margin on the sale of the product, depending on whether the drop shipper or middleman has to pay for the shipping costs. A small mail order dealer with a larger volume of orders drop shipped by the manufacturer may benefit from the lower shipping costs as compared with those of a dealer who stocks the merchandise and does their own shipping. There are no quantity discounts for the volume mailing of parcel post or UPS shipments. However, a manufacturer dealing in very heavy products that are shipped via motor freight may make substantial savings by combining drop shipped orders of several dealers and by using freight forwarders or freight consolidators.

SALES AGREEMENT BETWEEN THE DROP SHIPPER AND MIDDLEMAN

Manufacturers and distributors can use many methods such as direct mail, trade advertising in publications or personal selling to gain dealers. The net wholesale or dealer prices on merchandise are usually spelled out in the literature, indicating quantity discounts and f.o.b. point for sales to dealers that stock. In addition, the single-unit drop shipped prices are usually defined in such literature. Depending on the weight of the product, the drop shipper, as an example, might absorb the shipping costs of third-class mail by indicating an in-the-mail price for each single unit.

Third-class bulk mail rates based on weight are the same throughout the entire United States, and packages weighing under 15.9 ounces are adaptable to the practice of including shipping costs within the single-unit drop shipped price. Heavy merchandise that has shipping costs based on various parcel post or UPS zones would vary with each drop shipped order, and such costs are usually billed to the dealer. If the drop shipper requires cash-with-order terms on single-unit drop shipments, the shipping charges can be billed to the dealer separately, if they are not included in the drop shipped price.

The product literature of the drop shipper should also mention that orders will be shipped within a defined number of days or that the dealer will be notified of the exact date the order was drop shipped. The drop shipper should also be obligated to notify the dealer if there are any delays in order to allow the dealer to notify customers under the 30 Day Mail Order Rule of the FTC. If the drop shipper bills the dealer for shipping costs, the shipping date can be defined on the bill. The sales literature of the drop shipper should also include the cost of samples of the merchandise and availability of sales aids such as camera-ready art, advertisements, catalog sheets for dealer imprint or reprint along with the cost, if any, for these materials.

WRITTEN CONTRACTS BETWEEN DROP SHIPPERS AND MIDDLEMEN

When middlemen, including mail order firms receive product literature from manufacturers or stocking distributors that provide drop shipping services, most of the terms and conditions concerning drop shipped orders would be included. The written offer to drop ship single units of a product would indicate the single-unit drop shipped price and whether the price is in-the-mail or if shipping costs on drop shipped orders would be added and billed separately. The written offer would also spell out whether cash-with-order terms are required or whether credit terms and billing will be extended to the middleman, along with returned merchandise arrangements, cooperative money back guarantees, product liability insurance, and how the drop shipper will notify the middleman when individual drop shipped orders are filled.

If the terms and conditions of the drop shipper are relatively simple, the middleman could restate these factors in a letter to the drop shipper indicating that the offer made by the supplier is understood and binding. Some of the terms and conditions may be complicated by such factors as the use of color catalog transparencies, slides and other expensive graphic arts or the contract price for catalog sheets or minicatalogs for dealer imprint or reprint. When in doubt, contact an attorney to review all facets of the drop shipping arrangement and to help negotiate a formal written contract between the drop shipper and middleman.

5

Syndicated Catalogs and Graphics Provided by Drop Shippers

Firms that perform drop shipping services often provide many types of materials to aid dealers in selling products including syndicated catalogs, catalog sheets, sales literature, copy, advertisements, photos, slides, color separations or custom copy and graphic services. Anything within reason that the drop shipper can supply dealers to aid in selling products, in turn, aids the drop shipper. There are a number of variations as to what will be supplied to dealers, based on the marketing policy decisions of drop shippers.

CATALOG SYNDICATIONS

The dictionary defines a syndicate as "a group of persons or concerns who combine to carry out a particular transaction" as in a syndication. The producers of syndicated catalogs make them available to dealers, usually at a price, and the name and address of the dealer appears printed on the catalog or on the order form. Catalog syndications are often sponsored by a manufacturer but more often by a distributor who selects products, designs the catalog, writes the copy, prepares product photography and prints the catalogs.

SYNDICATED CATALOGS OF MANUFACTURERS

A manufacturer involved in a catalog syndication must usually produce a relatively wide variety of similar products. A firm that manufactures only two or three products may supply dealers with literature for imprint or reprint, but the number of items is too small to justify a catalog. However, a manufacturer with 200 different types of wall and desk clocks may produce a profitable syndicated catalog with a mail order format. The catalog would be available to dealers at a price per thousand, imprinted, with the name and address of the dealer, or blank, with the name to be imprinted by the dealer. The catalog is syndicated to the extent that it is made available to dealers, and the manufacturer drop ships all of the clocks listed in the catalog directly to the customers of the dealers. As an alternative, the manufacturer could require that the dealers stock inventory of the clocks, without any means of projecting the sales volume of any one clock. In anticipation of sales, a dealer might be required to stock at least six units of each clock, which would result in a relatively large inventory of 1,200 clocks, costing many thousands of dollars. Any unsold clocks would just remain on the shelf as distress merchandise or returned to the manufacturer for credit. Through drop shipping, however, a dealer can distribute the syndicated catalog and forward the orders to the manufacturer to be drop shipped from their large, centralized inventory.

In this example, the manufacturer of clocks may want to include small wooden racks or wall units to house the clocks but may not want to make or stock these products. All of the furniture in the catalog might be drop shipped by a furniture manufacturer. In this example, the catalog syndicator could have a mixture of products that they manufacture or stock, in addition to those that are drop shipped by another firm. The clock manufacturer is acting as a middleman as far as the furniture segment of the syndicated catalog is concerned.

CATALOG SYNDICATIONS OF MIDDLEMEN

The function of catalog syndication is more apt to take place when produced by a distributor because of the wide variety of products available. As an example, a distributor might specialize in fishing gear: rods, reels, clothing, folding boats, lures, hats and dozens of other products that might appeal to fishermen. The sources for the products listed in the syndicated catalog might include dozens of manufacturers in addition to direct importers that stock. The distributor could receive copy and photos from the supply source or produce the distributor's own product photography and copy in a mail order catalog format and offer the catalog to dealers at a price per thousand, imprinted with the name of the dealer. The fishing gear distributor can virtually shop the market for many thousands of products, and the merchandising and product selection skills of the distributor would probably result in greater success for the syndicated catalog than if a mail order dealer undertook to develop a similar catalog independently. The distributor would provide single-unit drop shipping services on all of the products in the catalog. There are literally hundreds of other types of product groups that could be promoted by distributors through catalog syndications.

SYNDICATED CATALOGS PRODUCED BY PRINTERS

Some distributors may be more interested in making a profit by selling syndicated catalogs than in any profit they might make by drop shipping orders. A few catalog syndicators are basically printers who produce millions of catalogs of gifts and other items—many of which are inexpensive, unbranded imports. The huge print runs in the production of the catalogs may allow the drop shipper to charge dealers from four to five times the cost of printing the catalog. The distributor has already made a profit, whether or not the dealer sends in any orders to be drop shipped. A dealer, after paying for the catalogs, must rent or use a mailing list and go to the expense of mailing the syndicated catalog to potential customers with the hope that sales will cover all costs and render a profit.

The question might arise as to why distributors would prefer to sell the syndicated catalogs, instead of mailing them out under their own name and making all the profit on the sale of the products featured in the catalog. The fact of the matter may be that the only profit in this type of syndication is made by the distributor through the sale of the syndicated catalogs and not the merchandise. Any dealer who is considering the use of a prepared syndicated catalog should be careful in evaluating the cost of the catalogs, the types of products, profit margins, retail prices and market segmentation possibilities along with the cost of distributing the catalogs before getting involved in purchasing syndicated catalogs.

CATALOG SYNDICATIONS FOR SPECIAL MARKETS

There are a number of refinements of catalog and catalog sheet syndications in the form of envelope stuffers, bounce backs, billing statement inserts for credit card holders and other types of direct mail produced for major retailers and organizations. As an example, a large credit card company may be offered a selection of pretested products that are available on a single-unit drop ship basis by a stocking distributor. In addition, the distributor may provide the graphics (mechanicals and color separations), which are used by the credit card company to purchase the printed matter, or the distributor could have the printing done for the credit card company. In either case, the name and address of the credit card company appears on the literature and order blank; all orders are sent to the distributor to be drop shipped; and the credit card company bills their retail customers for the orders.

In a slight variation of the same system, the distributor prints all of the literature with the distributor's own name and address and does all of the product fulfillment, while the credit card company gets a verified and audited statement of sales and percentage of the gross, but this system does not involve drop shipping since the orders are being sent to and filled by the distributor. The credit card company is placing the literature of the distributor in outgoing bills in consideration for a percentage of the gross sales.

A syndicated catalog could be used as a profit center for a large membership organization by selling products that appeal to the special interests of members; however, the management of the organization may not want to bother with seeking out product sources, printing catalogs or literature and may call upon a distributor who is willing to produce a catalog of items and provide drop shipping services.

CATALOG SYNDICATORS THAT DO NOT DROP SHIP

A further refinement of catalog syndication concerns firms that supply mail order catalogs to dealers but do not stock or drop ship any merchandise. The syndicator does the product research, contacts sources that agree to drop ship the products at set prices, and has the syndicated catalog printed by performing all production functions such as product photography, copy and graphics to print the catalog in a mail order format. The catalog syndicator supplies the dealers who purchase the catalogs with a master list of all of the manufacturers or stocking distributors who have agreed to drop ship the products listed in the catalog. In addition, the syndicator may charge the manufacturer or stocking distributors who have agreed to drop ship the products for "advertising space" in the catalog. The syndicator in fact may be a printer or have a contract with a printer to have the catalogs produced. The syndicator is compensated by selling catalogs at a profit to dealers and from possible advertising revenues from the firms that have agreed to drop ship the products listed in the catalog. When the dealer received orders, they are sent to the proper list of product sources that drop ship the merchandise.

Dealers should be aware that they should carefully examine all aspects of such a catalog syndication from a product, merchandising and profit potential standpoint, before getting involved with this type of catalog syndication. However, small to medium-sized dealers may benefit by avoiding the high costs of producing their own catalog. The syndicator has performed a research, product evaluation and selection function, in addition to arranging for all of the printed material. These services may be more cost effective and of more value to dealers who wish to participate in direct marketing promotions, without the direct costs of producing their own catalog.

PI PUBLISHING, RADIO AND TELEVISION

PI or "per inquiry" is a mail order marketing method that utilizes the drop shipping services of a manufacturer, book publisher or distributor. A publisher may have unsold, excess or remnant advertising space in a magazine that can be filled with "house ads" offering books or merchandise to their readers on a PI basis. All products are drop shippped by the supply source that pays nothing for the advertising, except that the advertiser earns a percentage of gross sales. Radio and cable TV in particular on occasion participate in PI arrangements as a means of generating additional income from advertising air time that would have otherwise remained unsold.

MULTIPURPOSE SALES LITERATURE PRODUCED BY DROP SHIPPERS

Quite a few manufacturers overlook the possibility of having their product literature serve several purposes: selling the features of the merchandise to middlemen in addition to becoming a graphic means of selling the product to the ultimate consumer through a flyer or circular suitable for imprint by a mail order firm. Product promotion literature, often produced in full color, may contain product descriptions that would appeal to the merchandise buyer of a mail order firm, but the copy, layout and graphics would not necessarily sell the product to the ultimate consumer. Such collateral sales literature, in the form of catalog sheets, flyers or circulars, is in effect directed to middlemen and often similar in content to trade magazine advertising.

Incorporated into such catalog sheets or circulars, the terms of sale may be listed, such as wholesale prices, quantity discounts, advertising allowances, delivery costs and drop shipping data. Such information on catalog sheets or product literature automatically eliminates the use of the material as a means of selling the product to the ultimate consumer. Since the production of catalog sheets or flyers can be expensive, sales literature could be designed in such a way as to be useful for selling the product to middlemen in addition to the ultimate consumer. The details concerning the terms of sale to middlemen can be printed separately, allowing the flexibility of making changes in the terms without the need for continually reprinting the literature.

If the circular may be used by a dealer to gain mail orders, a separate order blank with the name and address of the dealer can be included with the literature of the manufacturer, along with the price of the merchandise. By preparing sales literature from the standpoint of the ultimate consumer, the manufacturer is able to look beyond the immediate goal of selling middlemen or dealers. The literature then becomes a sales tool that a dealer may distribute to retail customers and can be of particular value to dealers who use the drop shipping services of the manufacturer or stocking entity.

If the literature is produced by a manufacturer for the promotional use of dealers, it is advisable to exclude the name and particularly the address of the manufacturer. Dealers may be hesitant to promote products through literature that contains the full name and address of the manufacturer. It would be easy for a competitor or a retail consumer to write directly to the manufacturer. Product source data are usually confidential and should be an asset held by the seller. In the event that the catalog sheets or flyers contain the name and address of the manufacturer, many dealers may place a label bearing their own name and address over that of the manufacturer, which is an unsightly practice, and the use of such labels gives the impression that something the retail consumer should know is being covered up.

Catalog sheets, circulars or catalogs that are blank as to the name and address of the manufacturer can be supplemented by a separate order form to be imprinted with the name of the dealer. If the literature is to be imprinted by a dealer on a local level, perhaps on a small offset press, the position of the space to be imprinted with the name and address of the dealer must coincide with the capabilities of the printing press. Single sheet flyers or circulars should be supplied to dealers flat because once the literature is folded, the material cannot be run through a printing press with ease. Some manufacturers may choose to print a portion of a press run of circulars with their own name and address and the balance of the run blank. The original negatives and offset plates contain the name of the manufacturer, and after a certain press run, the name can be removed directly from the offset plate while they are still on the press. If a mail order firm may want to order a large quantity of flyers printed by the manufacturer, the entire press run may contain the name and address of the dealer on the order form portion of the literature. In such cases, the dealer would pay for all printing costs.

The sales literature properly prepared by the manufacturer can be of better quality than the dealer or mail order firm may be capable of producing, particularly if the printing is in full color. It could be very costly for a dealer to produce a small press run of full color circulars. In one known example, a manufacturer sold 6 million four-color circulars to dealers, ready for their imprint on a local level. The manufacturer recovered all of the printing and shipping cost of the circulars, and the printed material was far less expensive than if the dealers had prepared and printed the literature themselves. The mail order dealers used the literature as package and catalog inserts and included the circulars in all other outgoing mail. The production and sale of literature to dealers was successful because advertising copy and graphics were carefully developed to sell the product to the ultimate consumer, with all orders going direct to the dealer. The manufacturer, in turn, provided full drop shipping services on single-unit orders.

If the contents of sales literature is such that the manufacturer may want to have the material protected under copyright law, it is possible to have legal copyright notice without using the the full name of the company as the copyright claimant. If the firm is generally known by initials or an abbreviation of the company name in a particular line of trade, then they may use the abbreviation on the copyright notice. The use of initials indicating a copyright notice is described in material supplied by the Publications Division, Register of Copyrights, Library of Congress, Washington, DC 20059. Through the use of initials, the manufacturer can gain protection under copyright law without the full disclosure of the complete company name.

PREPRICING PRODUCTS IN LITERATURE OF
DROP SHIPPERS

The FTC frowns on the practice of having the retail price of products indicated in literature or advertising that is printed or produced by the manufacturer. The use of the suggested retail price in such literature may have diminished, but there is still some use of prepricing of products on packaging. In an effort to avoid the problems of prepricing of products in sales literature created by the drop shipper, but to be printed by dealers, the retail prices of products are often omitted. The artwork suplied to the dealer by the drop shipper would indicate a space for the retail prices as $00.00, and the dealers would then add retail prices before printing the literature. If the product, as an example, has an in-the-mail drop shipped cost of $5 to a dealer, the retail price selected by the dealer may be between $10 and $15, at the option of the middleman and to conform with FTC regulations.

If the syndicated catalog or literature is preprinted with the retail prices by the manufacturer or drop shipper, the dealer using the literature may be required to state that the prices in the material were requested or agreed upon by the dealer. There would be no economies in large print runs for literature or syndicated catalogs if each dealer required the drop shipper to have different printed retail prices on the various products. Often the problem of retail prepricing of products in syndicated catalogs produced by the manufacturer or drop shipper is largely ignored. For syndicated catalogs printed in vast quantities and sold to dealers by drop shippers, the catalogs invariably have the retail prices of the products included in the printed matter. The only alternative would be to have the products described without retail prices and identified by a stock number to be listed and priced on a separate order blank that could be imprinted with the name of the dealer. In this case dealers could prepare their own order blanks, with retail prices of their own choosing.

PHOTOGRAPHY PROVIDED BY DROP SHIPPERS

Print media advertising, including catalogs, flyers and circulars, as well as magazine and newspaper ads, basically consists of two elements: copy, in the form of typography and product photos, and art. These elements can be arranged in a great many combinations to create a graphic presentation to sell products. The cost of original art for promotion can be prohibitive, except for a few areas of illustration and line art. The commercial artist is therefore more involved with type and the preparation of camera-ready mechanicals for various printing processes. Although artistic talents are used, the conceptualization of advertising and creative arrangement of typography and photos is usually the basis for direct response formats.

The highest level of creative talent in print media advertising is often shown in the trade or consumer advertising of the manufacturer of products. However, many small manufacturers cannot afford to produce consumer advertising to pull their products through a channel of distribution. If consumer product advertising is prepared by a middleman who uses the drop shipping services of the manufacturer, the middleman can control the content of printed material, including copy and product photography. In the case of direct response advertising, the mail order firm or middleman has the option of using or modifying advertising copy, photos or artwork supplied by the manufacturer. Direct response or mail order product promotion that is designed to sell products for future delivery increases the importance of good product photography. Unless the manufacturer is selling to the largest retailers, catalog houses, catalog syndicators or mail order firms that may have the ability and facilities to produce product photography, few mail order firms or middlemen will spend the time or money to produce original product photography. The selection of a product for promotion by a mail order firm is often based on the quality of the photography supplied by the manufacturer. If a manufacturer can supply good, clear black-and-white product photos, the chances are greatly increased that a middleman will promote the products of the manufacturer.

Middlemen trained in the art of selecting products must consider available photos from the viewpoint of the ultimate consumer. One of the problems in black-and-white photography lies in the fact that a photo may be reproduced in different sizes, by various printing processes and on paper of varying qualities. An 8 × 10 black-and-white photo of a product may look attractive but will not reproduce well when reduced to an 11-pica column width and printed on newspaper stock. All of the detail showing the appearance of the product may blend into a muddy halftone that is hardly distinguishable as a product. The same photo may need to be silhouetted, retouched or airbrushed to emphasize details when reproduced on newspaper-grade paper stock. Even better results may be gained if a line conversion, wood cut engraving, velox or special-effect screen print of the photo is available. However, this same 8 × 10 photo that has been prepared for small sized, newspaper stock reproduction may appear to be over-retouched and harsh when reproduced in a 5 × 7 size (2 column by 196 lines) on coated stock in a magazine.

Therefore, a manufacturer should have several black-and-white photos that are available for reproduction in various sizes and on different types of paper. A manufacturer that provides drop shipping services has a tremendous vested interest in having photos that will induce mail order firms and other middlemen who use drop shipping services of the manufacturer. The main concern of both the manufacturer and middleman is in the use of product photography as a selling tool. The function of drop shipping can only take place when products are sold for future delivery, and the best means by which a consumer can make a purchase decision is based on a picture of the product, modified by advertising copy.

Middlemen who use the drop shipping services of manufacturers often do not have the facilities for product photography and to a great extent will rely on photos supplied by the manufacturer. For the middleman, the cost of producing original photography may be prohibitive. On the other hand, the rotogravure catalogs of some large mail order firms that print millions of catalogs may depict every product photo with the same airbrush background, and all the photos will have the same treatment, retouching or style. Middlemen can then produce their own photographs with the net result that the catalog appears to have been created by one graphics designer.

Manufacturers or distributors who provide drop shipping services should make black-and-white photos of products available to middlemen without charge. Direct marketers may spend thousands of dollars in promoting the product of the manufacturer, however the decision to sell the product may be based on the availability of a good, suitable photo. If the manufacturer or drop shipper insists on charging for black-and-white photos, they should be offered at cost. However, 35mm Ektachrome slides or studio transparencies obviously cost the product source more than black-and-white photos. Transparencies could be on loan to the middleman for the preparation of advertising or sold at cost. A full set of four-color separation negatives would vary in cost, depending on the number of color transparencies, special rules, tints, butts, traps or special stripping for highly complex catalog or advertising graphics.

Color transparencies that may be supplied by the drop shipper to a middleman can usually pose more problems than black-and-white prints, particularly if several color photos of different manufacturers are composed on the same page. A catalog that has a page of color transparencies pro-

duced by five different photographers will lack uniformity of lighting and
treatment and may prevent the economies of gang separations. Large catalog syndicators or mail order firms could better afford the cost of having
all the products printed in color to be photographed by one person. The
resulting catalog would no doubt offer a more professional appearance.

ADVERTISING AND CATALOG COPY PROVIDED BY
DROP SHIPPERS

Manufacturers who provide drop shipping services also have a vested
interest in the advertising copy used to describe their products. Most manufacturers have written descriptions of the features of the product that can
be translated into advertising copy designed to sell the product, sight unseen, for future delivery through direct response marketing methods. The
constant refinement of copy by the manufacturer has probably eliminated
gross exaggerations concerning product benefits or unrealistic product
claims. Care in advertising copy preparation is especially critical in such
product classifications as health foods, vitamin supplements, weight-re-
ducing plans or product features that would affect the health or safety of
the user.

The manufacturer or middleman who provided drop shipping services
for other firms can supply suggested advertising or catalog copy in the form
of typewritten descriptions of various lengths or repro-quality copies of
typography. The manufacturer may also provide middlemen with complete
camera-ready artwork, with headlines, subheads and typeset copy in addition to an indication as to the position of photos. Such full-page mechanicals are helpful if the middleman plans to print a free-standing flyer or
circular. In this way, all of the typeset copy for the full-page circular would
be in the same type style and will offer a professional appearance.

If the products of several manufacturers are to be positioned on the same
page in a catalog, it is important to have all type set in the same style. In
this case, the repro copies of preset type supplied by individual manufacturers would be of little value, except as a guide for advertising copy
content. The direct marketer who is preparing a custom catalog has the
option of using the suggested advertising copy supplied by the manufacturer
or creating copy that would promote the total image and tone of the catalog.
To bring continuity to the catalog, it is usually desirable to have one creative
director or copywriter produce the written descriptions of each product.
In addition, varying amounts of space may be devoted to any one of five
or so products on a page. The catalog designer would have to determine
the space to be allowed for product photography or illustration, in addition
to the allocation of the space for copy. Adjustments to copy fitting, based
on the size allotment, can be made by use of different point sizes of the
same type face and possible changes in the leading between the lines.

Catalog production can be handled by the in-house art, copy or advertising departments of large middlemen or by one of many firms that specialize in the production of catalogs, including product photography and copy. The advisability of using catalog consultants would depend on the size of the print production order, the number of transparencies and the financial budget for producing the catalog. Manufacturers of most consumer and industrial products can offer a wide variety of advertising copy, photography, transparencies, camera-ready art or full-page advertisements that are available for use by middlemen and direct marketers in particular. Middlemen who use the drop shipping services of the manufacturer should request all available material for the preparation of advertising or catalogs.

6

Drop Shipper–Middleman Relations

SALES TERMS AND CONDITIONS OF DROP SHIPPERS

Whether a middleman uses the drop shipping services of existing suppliers or is seeking new product sources, the details as to the terms and conditions regarding orders handled by drop shippers should be clearly defined, preferably in writing. The product literature of the manufacturer or the price list of stocking distributors will usually indicate whether drop shipping services are offered. If the middleman is a retail mail order firm, their main interest would be the single-unit drop ship price for each product. As an example, a manufacturer or stocking distributor may state $20 as the single-unit drop shipped price for a product, in-the-mail, which includes shipping, order processing and handling costs.

If the product can be shipped by third-class merchandise rates, the cost of mailing is the same throughout the United States, and the drop shipper knows the exact shipping costs that can be included within the $20 in-the-mail drop shipped price. On parcel post, United Parcel Service or motor freight drop shipments, the cost of shipping would vary from one product to another, based on weight and destination. In this event, the drop shipper may still offer an in-the-mail price on drop shipments by including an average shipping cost for all destinations which is figured into the $20 drop shipped cost to middlemen. The fixed drop shipped price, regardless of the destination, is convenient when cash-with-order terms are required by the drop shipper, and it is not necessary to bill middlemen for shipping charges.

In this example, the drop shipper could also indicate that a shipping and handling charge of $3 per unit would be added to the basic cost of $20 for the product. The $3 charge would offset the costs of shipping, which might vary depending on the destination of the shipment. In effect, the drop shipper has segmented the costs for middlemen by defining the drop shipped price of $20 for the product, plus $3 for shipping and handling, resulting in a total cost of $23 per unit, in-the-mail. On heavy products, the drop shipper may offer a slightly modified arrangement in that cash-with-order would be required with each drop shipped order, with the exact shipping costs to be billed to the middleman. The drop shipper has payment in full for the merchandise immediately, with the shipping costs to be paid by the middleman monthly, based on an invoice that would identify each drop shipped order, the date shipped, and the cost of parcel post, UPS or motor freight charges. Depending on the credit rating of the middleman, the drop shipper could also offer to accept orders on open account by which the middleman would send a written purchase order to the drop shipper, along with preaddressed shipping labels coded for the type and quantity of the product. The drop shipper would fill all orders as they are received, and by billing the middleman on a monthly basis, a great deal of paperwork could be eliminated.

CONFIDENTIALITY OF CUSTOMER LIST OF MIDDLEMEN

The relationship between middlemen and drop shippers is one of a private contract between two business entities, as defined in letters from the Federal Trade Commission which are reproduced in chapter 2 of this book. Some ethical factors may go beyond a written contract, however, in that the drop shipper has possession of the names and addresses of the customers of the middleman who initiates drop ship orders. Because the manufacturer or stocking distributor performs drop shipping services, it is unlikely that they would attempt to sell to the same customers. If that were the case, the drop shipper would become a direct competitor of the middleman. It is a trade practice, therefore, and often part of a contract that the drop shipper will not use, rent or solicit orders from the customer lists of the middlemen they supply.

In addition, drop shippers should not place literature in any of the packages of drop shipped merchandise that promote the business interests of the drop shipper. The middlemen can request that their own catalog or sales material be placed in the packages of their drop shipped orders. The only literature the manufacturer would normally include in the merchandise package are the instructions for use, directions for assembly, warranty and service or product guarantee cards, which are often contained in the factory-sealed cartons, which would normally be mailed back to the manufacturer by the ultimate consumer. A written agreement between the middleman and the drop shipper should define what will be placed in the packages of drop shipped orders, such as literature, acknowledgements, packing slips or invoices that may be provided by the middleman.

EXISTING SUPPLIERS AS DROP SHIPPERS

Established middlemen have no doubt developed relationships with manufacturers or distributors that are a source of supply for products, and under ordinary circumstances the middleman would stock merchandise inventory. If a middleman can sell these same products for future delivery to customers, they have the option of having the products drop shipped by their current sources, if these manufacturers or stocking distributors will in fact provide drop shipping services. Many manufacturers and distributors will not indicate in their regular product literature or price lists that they will drop ship products. The lack of reference to drop shipping in the literature of manufacturers or distributors may indicate that they do not drop ship orders under any circumstances. However, they may provide such services, if a middleman specifically requests drop shipping.

Although drop shipping services may not be generally promoted, if a manufacturer or distributor does provide drop shipping service for one middleman, they would be required to perform this same service for all middlemen to conform with the conditions of the Robinson-Patman Act. Unless drop shipping information is clearly defined in the literature, the only way to determine whether a product source will drop ship orders would be to direct a letter of inquiry to the sales or marketing manager of the supplier. An example of a possible letter of inquiry to manufacturers or distributors that are current sources of merchandise follows:

We have been ordering and stocking numerous products [list, if necessary] from your company. We are expanding our direct mail/direct marketing advertising and sales efforts which will include your products. However, the bulk of these sales will be in the form of mail orders that would allow the products to be drop shipped by your firm, rather than our stocking the merchandise for reshipment to our customers. Please let us know if you will drop ship single units (or in quantity) of the above products direct to our customers under shipping labels that we would supply. Please send us complete cost data, terms and conditions regarding single-unit drop shipments of your products.

Based on the response from the product sources, the middleman could compare all of the costs of stocking inventory of the products with the prices quoted on drop shipments by the manufacturer or stocking entity. The single-unit drop ship prices may appear on the surface to be higher than the unit cost of the products, if they were stocked in quantity. As an example, the single-unit drop shipped price of a product may be $20 in-the-mail, and the same product might have a single-unit cost of $17 if the middleman stocked the item in gross quantities. Although it would require a detailed cost accounting procedure, it might be determined that the total pro rata share of overhead costs by stocking the same single unit of the product, including the shipping costs to the customer of the middleman, might be $7 or $8 per unit or $24 to $25 each, as compared with the $20 in-the-mail, single-unit drop shipped price offered by the manufacturer.

NEW SUPPLIERS AS DROP SHIPPERS

Most middlemen, whether they are wholesalers, retailers or mail order firms, sell related groups of products such as sporting goods, toys, housewares, clothing or the hundreds of other types of similar products. The middlemen who presently stock inventories of sporting goods, as an example, may want to expand the number of sporting goods products in their line or add other types of items that would be compatible with the type of merchandise currently being sold. Middlemen would usually write letters of inquiry to either prime manufacturers, direct importers or stocking distributors to gain literature and the wholesale cost data on various products that would be stocked as inventory by the middleman. Information should also be requested on drop shipping services that may be offered by the supply source, along with the cost of single- and multiple-unit drop shipments of the products offered. Several possible letters of inquiry could be composed as follows:

> We are direct marketers of sporting goods through our mail order catalog, distributed in quantities of 100,000 twice a year. We are seeking additional products for our next catalog and would appreciate receiving literature on all of your products, along with terms, quantity discounts and conditions of sale. We would also appreciate knowing the costs of drop shipments of single and multiple units of your products, direct to our customers under our preaddressed shipping labels, if you provide drop shipping services.

> We are wholesalers of general merchandise, servicing retailers in the New England area. Please send us literature on your various products, along with quantity discounts offered to wholesalers, terms and conditions of sale. Also, we would appreciate knowing if you will drop ship single units or various quantities of your products, direct to our retail store customers, under our shipping labels. Please include complete details and prices on drop shipped products, if you provide this service.

> We are distributors of industrial cutting tools and abrasives selling direct to hundreds of East Coast companies. We are interested in expanding our product line and would appreciate receiving distributors' pricing on your products (power tools, lubricants, drills or other similar lines), along with

literature. In addition, we would appreciate knowing if you will drop ship products direct to our industrial customers, under our preaddressed shipping labels. Please send full data and cost information on the products that your firm may drop ship.

There are numerous variations as to the composition of letters of inquiry to product sources, all of which should be modified by the type of business of the middleman. In all cases it would be advisable to request cost data on products as if they were to be stocked by middlemen, in addition to the costs of drop shipped orders, so that a comparison can be made between the two options. If the middleman produces a substantial volume of business, the dollar volume of sales might be mentioned in the letter of inquiry to the drop shipper or an indication as to their impressive number of customers or employees. Once the basic data are received from product sources, the middleman can request specific details on the availability of product photos, advertising copy, camera-ready artwork or type, color transparencies or literature for imprint or reprint. Other aspects of the drop shipping arrangement can be determined such as the procedure for filling drop shipped orders, the means for handling defective merchandise, co-op refunds, product guarantees and the inclusion of any literature of the middleman in the drop shipped merchandise packages. These aspects of the terms and conditions for handling orders may be the basis for a written contract between the middleman and the drop shipper.

MAIL ORDER FIRMS: LETTERS OF INQUIRY TO DROP SHIPPERS

Selling by mail, by mail order or by the currently popular term *direct response marketing* provides an ideal basis for the use of drop shipping as a marketing function. Products sold for future delivery to consumers through mail order marketing methods, direct mail, advertisements in publications, catalogs or electronic media provide the conditions that allow merchandise to be drop shipped by a manufacturer or stocking distributor. Letters of inquiry from mail order companies that are seeking product sources on a drop ship basis are similar to those composed by any other type of middleman, but the fact that the products will be sold by mail order is often included in the letter of inquiry. The mail order firm may be in existence and have produced a catalog, used direct mail or placed mail order advertisements in publications, or the mail order company may be a new business without having produced any product promotion materials. The contents of letters of inquiry to prospective product sources may vary, depending on the type or status of the mail order firm. A letter of inquiry from an existing mail order firm might be composed as follows:

We are seeking additional products for inclusion in our next mail order catalog [optional, include a copy of the current catalog] and through advertisements in various publications. Please send us literature on all of your products, including net mail order distributor pricing, quantity discounts, packaging, terms and conditions of sale. Since we are selling products for future delivery by mail order, we would appreciate knowing if you will drop ship single units of your products directly to our retail customers under our shipping labels. Please include complete details and prices on the products that you will drop ship.

The previous letter could also give the number of catalogs printed for past promotions, the volume of direct mail sent per year, sales volume, number of employees, D-U-N-S (number) assigned by Dun and Bradstreet, Inc. or any other information that may indicate to the potential supply source that the mail order firm would be capable of promoting the products of the manufacturer.

A letter of inquiry for a new mail order firm might be composed as follows:

We are in the process of seeking product sources for a new mail order catalog [optional, quantity to be printed, number of pages, four-color or black/white, etc.] to be produced in [two months, four months, etc.]. Please send us literature on all of your products, indicating net mail order distributor pricing, quantity discounts, packaging, along with terms and conditions of sale. Since we are selling products for future delivery by mail order, we would also appreciate knowing if your firm will drop ship single units of your products to our customers under our shipping labels. Please indicate net prices for single-unit drop shipments on all your products, with in-the-mail pricing or data on shipping costs.

RESPONSE TO INQUIRIES

One would think that every manufacturer or stocking distributor of products would be anxious to sell their products to virtually any firm that professes to have an ability or interest in selling products. However, the relationship between a middleman and supply source is initially voluntary. A manufacturer is under no obligation to respond to letters of inquiry from potential dealers, nor are they obligated to sell products to every firm that inquires about their line. The manufacturer or distributor is usually continually trying to sell products, however middlemen also must make the effort to "sell" the source of supply of the products that they are a firm worthy and capable of selling the products.

The initial letter of inquiry from a middleman to a potential product source should therefore be concerned with basic information. It is usually not advisable to request a long list of data from the supply source, at least in the first letter of inquiry. There are those who would be tempted to request glossy photos of all the products, samples, color transparencies, data on how long the products will be in stock, whether the names of drop ship customers will be protected, whether the middleman can sell below the suggested retail price, how many shipping labels are required on drop shipped orders, the suggested retail price on all products or other questions that go far beyond any realistic initial purpose. Most manufacturers would not respond to letters that would require answers to this list of questions.

The answers to the questions just listed would no doubt be of value to the middleman, however this line of inquiry may be premature. Initial letters of inquiry from middlemen to potential supply sources might be best designed to obtain all of the existing literature on the products manufactured by the source, wholesale costs, and information on the products that they are willing to drop ship. Some supply sources may not be willing to supply all the details of in-the-mail drop shipped costs for all their products in reply to an initial letter of inquiry. Also, the supply source may not have or may not be willing to supply glossy photos or samples of the products they manufacture. In addition, many supply sources may not have drop shipping information printed in their regular product literature and would be willing to offer this specific information on only a few products. Letters of inquiry from middlemen to potential product sources should allow the respondent the flexibility to supply whatever product literature is available. If the middleman would want to promote several of the products of a specific manufacturer, then the additional information and answers to the previous questions can be determined through a follow-up letter to the supply source. Once the supply source has agreed to supply the middleman, an implied or written contract is usually the result, and the middleman would want written assurance as to how long the product would be available and that the drop shipped single-unit price would be the same for six months to a year.

INITIATING DROP SHIPPED ORDERS BY MIDDLEMEN

The method of placement of orders by middlemen to be drop shipped by a stocking entity may vary, based on the volume of orders and the availability of various types of equipment. In most instances, orders are drop shipped under the preaddressed shipping labels that are typed or prepared by the middleman and are often supplied to the drop shipper in duplicate. Other order placement systems may include the use of personal computers or word processors that will generate a printout based on stored codes as to the name and address of the drop shipper and codes for the product and drop shipped price. The result is a purchase order that includes a shipping label, in addition to the direct entry of the order transaction into the computer-based accounting system of the middleman. Depending on the distance to the supply source, the middleman could also phone the drop shipped order to the supplier, to be followed by a written order. In this case, the middleman would give the drop shipper a supply of shipping labels which would be prepared from the telephone order. Other systems might use FAX in combination with shipping label preparation by the drop shipper. Orders prepared by the middleman are usually mailed daily to the drop shippers and include cash-with-order, if required by the drop shipper.

NOTIFYING MIDDLEMEN OF ORDER FULFILLMENT DATE

Middlemen who initiate drop ship orders should be notified immediately by the drop shipper as to the date the product is shipped to the customer of the middleman. Notification of shipping date should be sent to the middleman on both cash-with-order drop shipments and those on open account. Although open account billing by the drop shipper may indicate the date an order was drop shipped, the middleman may only receive the billing statement once a month. If the bill for the merchandise was the only method of notifying the middleman of the shipping date, the shipment of an order early in the billing cycle may not be known to the middleman for twenty to twenty-five days after shipment was made. To avoid this problem, many middlemen supply the drop shipper with self-addressed postcards with the date of shipment to be filled in by the drop shipper.

A middleman may mail a merchandise order to the drop shipper on the first of the month. The order is generally received on the third, and the order filled within one or two days. The date the drop shipper fills the order is important since the middleman wants assurance that the order was in fact filled on a specific date and not back-ordered. If the drop shipper, for some unlikely reason, is out of stock, the expected date of shipment should also be sent to the middleman.

The date a drop ship order is filled is related to the 30 Day Mail Order Rule of the Federal Trade Commission, since it is the responsibility of the middleman to notify customers if the product cannot be shipped within the thirty-day period, and this information is only available from the drop shipper. As mentioned in the letters from the FTC in chapter 2, the entire responsibility for shipment or notification rests with the middleman and not the drop shipper.

GUARANTEES AND REFUNDS SHARED BY MIDDLEMEN AND DROP SHIPPERS

Co-op guarantees on defective merchandise are often part of the agreed upon terms and conditions of sale between middlemen and the drop shipper. If a faulty product is drop shipped to the customer of the middleman, the customer would normally return the defective product to the middleman who sold the product to the customer. As an example, if a product retails for $20 and the drop shipped, in-the-mail price charged by the drop shipper to the middleman is $10, the middleman must make a direct refund of the total sale price of $20 to the customer. The defective product under most circumstances would be returned to the drop shipper by the middleman for a credit in the amount of $10. The middleman has shared the cost of $10 as part of the refund, and the drop shipper extends a credit of $10 on future orders placed by the middleman.

Most middlemen involved in direct marketing or mail order offer products to retail consumers on a money back or satisfaction guaranteed basis. If a customer returns a product to the middleman for a refund, and the item is still in salable condition, the middleman would more than likely retain the product and resell it to the next customer who ordered the product. A small volume of money back guarantee requests would not be worth the cost to return salable products to the drop shipper. The details of co-op refunds on defective merchandise and the method for handling returned products under a money back guarantee should be clearly understood by both the middleman and drop shipper and should be part of a written contract between both companies.

Service on product warranties would normally be handled by the manufacturer, since either written or implied warranties are normally the responsibility of the producer of the product and not the middleman. This fact would also be true if the retail customer purchased the product over-the-counter from a department store or appliance dealer. The numbered warranty card, with the name of the retailer, serial number of the item, date of purchase and other information required are usually sent to the manufacturer on a preprinted guarantee or warranty. In the case of an adjustment or repair of a defective product under warranty, the retail customer would usually return the merchandise directly to the manufacturer or a designated service company. There is usually no reason for the middleman to become involved in the problems of handling complaints or returned items under a warranty issued by the manufacturer. If the product is by chance returned to the middleman by the customer who is requesting repair or replacement under a warranty issued by the manufacturer, the middleman can only comply by reshipping the product to the manufacturer and then notifying the consumer to that effect.

7

Direct Marketing Guidelines and Product Evaluations for Mail Order Promotions

GUIDELINES FOR DIRECT MARKETING

Although there are many books on mail order and direct response marketing, some do not review basic guidelines for the formation of a new mail order company or a new mail order division of an existing firm. Missing too is a discussion of product selection and evaluation, market and media segmentation, and the criteria for selling products for future delivery, along with the use of drop shipping as a marketing function. Some mail order firms have vast experience in selecting and marketing products for future delivery, while other middlemen have only sold products over-the-counter but may be considering selling by mail order. Other mail order firms may be newly formed, based on the relatively low capital investment necessary, particularly if the products are drop shipped by the manufacturer or stocking distributors. This chapter discusses some of the guidelines for selling products for future delivery, particularly from the standpoint of a new mail order business.

CREATING CONSUMER CONFIDENCE: ALL IN A NAME

Most businesses select names that will create a favorable impression on customers, and names are often chosen based on tradition, custom or without much planning at all. A company name can have an impact on how the public perceives the firm, particularly in the area of direct marketing. Along with all the elements of direct response advertising in the form of direct mail, catalogs, advertisements in publications or electronic media, the public is buying products sight unseen based on product ad copy, graphics and price. The consumer is also buying the image or reputation of the company name, which in all cases should attempt to create consumer confidence. No rules govern the choice of company name, except for possible infringements on the name of another company or other legal considerations. The register of business trade styles or state corporate charter registrations will reveal possible conflicts. In most cases an attorney should be used to register a company name, business trade style or corporate charter. The choice of a company name is particularly important to direct marketers.

The bulk of all products are sold through middlemen who stock goods. Retail consumers must therefore visit the seller's store or place of business. The company name is then modified by the appearance of the store, the merchandise displays, the helpfulness of clerks and the general tone of the establishment. Obviously, the retail consumer can gain a great insight into the nature of the firm, and consumer confidence can be built firsthand. Not so in direct response marketing, since all efforts to sell products and create consumer confidence must rely on the name of the company and the merits of the products sold, along with advertising designed to create a favorable image.

Direct marketers can use an abstract group of letters, coined words, words modified by the type of products sold or the name of a person or persons. There are advantages and disadvantages of these possibilities. A direct response marketer could have originally been conceived as an importer. But if the company also deals in exports, it might not be appropriate to call the firm ABS Import-Export. If all of their customers are domestic retail consumers in the United States, they would have little interest in whether the firm exported products to foreign countries. In addition, a retail consumer may prefer not to deal with a firm that is involved in imports or exports. The inclusion of the terms import, export, wholesale or distributor defines the type of business activity, rather than the merchandise sold. A company name could include the general classification of products sold, such as AZ Housewares, ABC Sporting Goods or PR Hardware. A product specialty within a company name may create consumer confidence, but this factor may restrict expansion into another product line in the future.

In many businesses, large or small, the name of the owners or founders may be the choice of a company name. Anyone close to advertising would know that J. Walter Thompson, McCann Erickson and Benton & Bowles are among the largest advertising agencies in the country. The names of advertising agencies are generally unknown to the public, but this is of little consequence because the advertising agencies are really only concerned with doing business with the advertising managers of very large companies. Based on the use of the individual names of the persons who founded these advertising agencies, any of these firms could be a law or

CPA firm as far as the general public is concerned. Sears Roebuck & Co., on the other hand, would be immediately recognizable as a retailer and direct marketer. This company name has become a household word because of the millions of dollars spent on advertising and mail order catalogs over the years, along with their very large retail store operation. In the final analysis, a company name should be chosen to closely match what is felt will make the best impression on customers in the long term.

Aside from direct marketing companies, the products or services offered by some of the largest firms may change, or management may feel that the original company name was too long, too short, too descriptive or not descriptive enough. It can be costly to change or rebuild a company and identity many years after the original company name was chosen. Yet literally hundreds of examples of such changes have been recorded over the past years: American Machine & Foundry to AMF, Cities Service to Citgo, Liggett & Meyers Tobacco Co. to The Liggett Group, Addressograph-Multigraph to AM International and dozens more. In some cases the firm wanted to shorten the company name; in others to deemphasize a type of product; in others to shift emphasis from tobacco to another group of consumer products or to eliminate a function performed, as in the case of the nonexistent foundry at AMF.

Existing firms obviously have names, however there are means for altering or modifying the image of a firm by establishing separate divisions or business trade style. In many states a corporation can do business under an assumed name. As an example, *Drop Shipping News* has been registered as an assumed name by Consolidated Marketing Services, Inc., which protects the ownership of the name of the publication without the formation of a separate corporation. If a company name contains words that already define a service or product group, little can be done to modify the name, however the initials of the company can often be used, or the terms mail order, import or export divisions can be added to letterheads. The selection of the name of a new mail order firm should be chosen with care.

PRODUCT EVALUATIONS FOR MAIL ORDER PROMOTION

Perhaps the most difficult marketing decision lies in the evaluation of a product or a group of products to advertise or promote through direct response advertising. The costs of advertising space, postage and printing are increasing every year, making the product choice even more important. Almost every product manufactured has some unique features. The major difficulty concerns an attempt to determine whether a product can be sold profitably through direct marketing. A great many initial marketing decisions and product selections are made on the basis of insight and experience. Some individuals have a feel for a product as to whether the item can be sold in enough volume to justify placement in a catalog or space

advertising in various publications. Product selection decisions based on
intuitive insight can be a valid start. The product features, relative to
advertising and media promotion possibilities, can often be visualized, in
addition to the evaluation of the potential market for a product. Successful
merchandisers on a retail store level have demonstrated this same insight
into product evaluations, selection and promotion. The basis for many of
the subjective factors that surround product values applicable to direct
marketing are as follows:

Exclusivity

Specialty products, or those that have appeal other than price, are perhaps the best candidates for direct response or mail order promotion. Since
specialty products are usually not available in every retail store, the lack
of mass distribution tends to give a product an exclusive status in the
marketplace. If a product is easily accessible in every corner outlet, there
is hardly any real incentive for a retail consumer to order the product for
future delivery, unless there are other factors involved, such as a substantial
cost saving. A product that is customized, personalized and available only
by mail or is in limited distribution can create a form of exclusivity.

Eye appeal

The "eye of the beholder" allows an unlimited array of opinions and
judgments about almost anything. In the fashion industry or in areas where
a product is stylized, there are those who can predict to a degree what
products will be successful. The creative talents of the designer can be the
key factor as to whether a product can be sold based on its appearance,
color, texture and function.

Uniqueness

While the exclusivity of a product refers to restrictive or selective distribution and its availability in the marketplace, the uniqueness of an item
indicates product features that will differentiate the product from all others.
Product features can be patented, indicating true utility or uniqueness
based on the design or manufactured form of the product, as opposed to
all other products. Unique product features are perhaps the greatest factor
that will allow a product to be sold profitably. The evaluation of the unique
features of a product are subjective in that they involve personal opinions,
based on the evaluation of the product features, relative to the different
features of other similar products. A great deal of all mail order or direct
response advertising is based on an attempt to convince the buying public

that the unique features of the product are better or are of more value than the features of competing products.

Obvious value

Another subjective or opinion-oriented benchmark that is applied to most products is the value of the item. What may be of value to one consumer may be of little value to another. The obvious value of a product is usually a personal conviction of the potential buyer. In selecting products for promotion, the direct marketer must look at product features, benefits and value through the eyes of the buyer. Products that have the best chance of successful sales through mail order methods are those that have obvious value, based on product features and price.

Utility

Closely akin to obvious value is the utility of a product. While obvious value relates to the features and price of a product, relative to other products, the utility of a product is a subjective factor concerning the ability of a product to satisfy consumer wants. Will it perform a useful purpose, regardless of the value or price that is placed on the product? The criteria for utility concerns the satisfaction of consumer needs or the intrinsic qualities of product attributes from the standpoint of the consumer.

MAIL ORDER PRODUCT EVALUATION

Many of the previously discussed factors could be used as a guide for buying decisions by the merchandise manager of a department store or other retailer. The factors mentioned can also be directly applicable as a guide for product selection for direct response advertising promotion; however, products selected for direct response or mail order must undergo many more tests for acceptability. A retail store customer who is purchasing merchandise can see, feel, touch and evaluate a product firsthand, by physical examination. The merchandise buyer of a department store relies on the concept that when a potential customer sees the product physically, all of the factors going into a decision to purchase the product will be easier than if a consumer saw the same product promoted in a mail order advertisement. Unconsciously the retail customer makes a continual array of product evaluations before buying the product. The appearance of the product is measured against the individual needs of the buyer through the eye appeal, uniqueness, obvious value and utility of the product.

Through direct response or mail order marketing, all the tactile and visual benefits of allowing the consumer to see the product firsthand in a store must be portrayed through graphic or electronic representation, in addition to persuasive advertising copy to stimulate a direct response (i.e., the purchase of the product sight unseen for future delivery). The gap between the physical examination of the product by the consumer as a means for making a buying decision and the purchase of the product based on an advertisement in a magazine or by direct mail must be bridged by marketing skills of the highest level. The photography, copy and graphic presentation of the product must be powerful enough to substitute for the consumer's physical examination of the product in a retail store.

The product evaluation process for direct marketers must be based on an opinion as to how all the physical as well as subjective values of the product can be depicted in an advertising message that can sell products sight unseen. One product that can be sold in a retail store may be difficult to photograph or describe. Another may have a color, texture or physical property that can only be measured by physical examination. Perhaps these products are not likely candidates for direct response marketing. Another product could lie on a retail store shelf for months but may have attributes best described through advertising copy, photography and graphics making it suitable for a successful direct response marketing program.

Some products can be sold through either direct response advertising or regular "indirect" response or retail store advertising. The average newspaper advertisement for housewares in a department store usually contains the silhouetted photos of fifteen to twenty products, side by side, in uniform spaces with some advertising copy: XYZ hair dryer, $14.95; ABC toaster, $9.98; PQR steam iron, $12.50, and so on. The photographic reproduction on newspaper stock is poor, and the copy and graphic reproduction is of low quality. The purpose of this type of retail store advertising is to get the consumer to come into the store to see, feel or evaluate the product firsthand and then make a purchase. Many of these same types of products could no doubt be sold through direct response or mail order advertising with the proper photography, media, copy and graphic presentation.

Direct marketers who promote completely unknown products, which lack any prior consumer awareness through the advertising efforts of the manufacturer, have the task of identifying the product through compelling photography, artwork and expansive advertising copy that is sufficient to inform the potential customer of product features and benefits. In effect, the entire burden of selling a virtually unknown product to the public depends on the graphics and copy of the advertising or catalog presentation of the direct marketer. Each direct marketer has to determine the merits of selling nationally known brands or other unbranded merchandise.

PROMOTION OF NATIONAL BRANDS OR
UNBRANDED MERCHANDISE

The catalogs and print media advertising of many national mail order marketers carry gift items or relatively unknown brands of products. The bulk of these gift items do not have any identification as to the manufacturer, and the only description of the products is conveyed through photos and advertising copy. These items such as lamps, novelties, glassware, clothing, household products, home decorations and jewelry usually do not have any indicated trademark or other identification.

While there is no doubt that unbranded merchandise can be sold by mail order or direct mail, the consumer is unfamiliar with the product source and may make extra effort to evaluate the products and their features, relative to the price of the items, before making a decision to purchase. Aside from mail order, this evaluation of unbranded products is often difficult for a consumer, even if the customer is in a retail store and can see, feel, operate and physically examine the product before making a purchase. The consumer may not have any means of making a realistic comparison of the product with other similar items, based on the product features and price, particularly if there is no brand name on the merchandise.

Many of these products are successfully sold through mail order marketing methods because the potential customer can see the obvious merit, usefulness or artistic value of the item, even though the products do not carry identification such as Sunbeam, GE, Toro, Black & Decker, AMF, Westinghouse, or the names of any other nationally known manufacturer of consumer goods. A great number of products sold successfully by mail are unidentified as to the manufacturer, particularly if they are imported. Unbranded products also make it very difficult for potential competitors to find out the source of a product that appears to be successful. In some nationally known mail order catalog firms that print virtually tens of millions of catalogs yearly, the vast majority of all the products promoted are unbranded merchandise imported from foreign countries at very low prices.

Nationally known brands of products that are manufactured in the United States usually are supported by huge advertising expenditures by the manufacturer in an effort to pull their products through a channel of distribution that normally stocks merchandise—for example, a retail store. In addition, nationally known manufacturers of such products as housewares, sporting goods, photographic equipment, consumer electronics and appliances may provide co-op advertising allowances, rebates, extra goods or other sales promotion methods to induce a department store, as an example, to feature their products in local newspaper advertising—all of which is designed to motivate consumers to come into the retail store and buy the advertised products.

Many national mail order companies overlook the possibility of promoting branded products through mail order marketing methods. Perhaps these mail order firms believe that the competition is too great to sell nationally known brands, or there can be more profit in promoting unknown specialty products that have appeal other than price. In addition, mail order firms may believe that the nationally advertised brands are too accessible, by being available in every corner drugstore, discount house, catalog showroom or department store in the country. Universal availability may have caused the conversion of these products from a "shopping" to a "convenience" good. The former being an item that motivates the consumer to shop around for the product from store to store, comparing prices and product features, and the later, a product of such universal availability and relative sameness in retail pricing that there is no incentive to shop for the item in various stores. Accordingly, the consumer can select the most convenient outlet that has an inventory of the item on hand and buy it.

The marketer who sells goods for future delivery through mail order methods is confronted with the decision as to whether unbranded or lesser known products should be advertised and sold or whether nationally known brands of merchandise can be profitably advertised and promoted. Few rules govern the selection of products for mail order promotion because a great deal of the decision-making process is based on the opinions of the management of the mail order firm as to the types of items than can be sold to a specific market. Product and advertising testing is perhaps the only method to determine whether one type of product, branded or unbranded, can be successfully sold for future delivery.

The possible advantages of promoting specialty or unbranded merchandise are based on the fact that the ultimate consumer may not have seen the product in retail stores, or in some instances the product may be new and not available in retail stores. The product may also be of excellent quality but may have appeal to a relatively small market and have distribution through a limited number of retail outlets. As an example, maybe only a few outlets in a large metropolitan area carry riding crops and horse blankets, and it may be easier for a consumer to order these types of products from a mail order catalog than to take the time to travel to a specialty store.

The other aspects of unbranded or specialty products concern the features of the products which can be so outstanding that the consumer can see the obvious value and worth of the items. The fact that the product is not manufactured by a nationally recognizable company may be an advantage as far as the consumer is concerned. Specialty clothing in the form of sportswear, shoes or boots that are produced by a small manufacturer may have greater appeal to the ultimate consumer than those produced by a major or nationally known maker. A designer fashion accessory such as a scarf that is outwardly identified as that of a nationally known brand name may or may not be an attractive feature, while a Wilson racket may be impressive on the tennis court. There is a place for nationally known, lesser known and unbranded products in direct response marketing; however there are numerous opportunities to promote nationally known products, especially since many of the large catalog houses appear to ignore this possibility.

If a direct marketer is of the opinion that nationally known brands are too widely available, this factor may be turned into an advantage. If a relatively unknown mail order company offers famous brand-named products at competitive prices by direct mail or through mail order advertising, the prestige, success, quality and image of the nationally known manufacturer is a positive reflection on the seller. The potential consumer would have a greater knowledge of the manufacturer than the firm selling the product. In addition, the consumer more than likely has already examined the style or model of the product in a local store before ordering by mail. The impact of nationally known brands in consumer electronics can be seen in the mail order ads in various audio or video magazines. The only description that appears to be needed is the name of the manufacturer, the model number and the price. The consumer has relatively full knowledge of the features of a specific VCR, TV set or stereo system and, in effect, can shop for the best price from various advertisements.

Many of the mail order firms offering consumer electronics will accept credit card orders by mail or 800 number, and there is a good possibility that the products are drop shipped to their customers in double-boxed, factory-sealed cartons from a regional distributor of consumer electronics products. By promoting the nationally known brand with stock or model number, many of the barriers that may prevent a consumer from ordering merchandise by mail may be reduced or eliminated, and if the price of the products is competitive, there is no reason why a consumer would hesitate to order a nationally known brand by mail. The time delay in receiving the product may not be any longer than if the item was shipped by UPS or truck from a local retailer. The consumer has eliminated a trip to the retailer by ordering by mail.

However, not all manufacturers of nationally advertised consumer products will drop ship single units of merchandise or drop ship in quantity for that matter. The marketing management of some large manufacturers of nationally known brands will only sell to wholesalers or distributors that stock merchandise in quantity or sell to a combination of wholesalers and distributors in addition to direct sales to large retailers, chains or national accounts. Mail order firms that are seeking drop shipping sources for some of these nationally known brands may have to rely on distributors or large wholesalers as a supply source.

DIRECT AND INDIRECT RESPONSE ADVERTISING

Mail order direct marketers may benefit from the general or indirect response advertising of consumer product manufacturers as a means for preselling potential buyers of products, particularly if the manufacturer produces name-brand merchandise. Some mail order marketers hesitate in selling products produced by major manufacturers such as consumer electronics, sporting goods and photographic equipment. As an example, one of the world's largest manufacturers of cameras and projectors spends a great deal of money on consumer product advertising, in addition to offering mail order firms or catalog showrooms drop shipping services on single units of product. The camera manufacturer indicated through trade magazine advertising that a large group of potential retail buyers will be exposed to a vast amount of consumer advertising in magazines, newspapers and on radio and television. The manufacturer is spending advertising dollars in an effort to help retailers have a successful sales year, in addition to encouraging the middlemen to include the camera line in catalogs. The consumer advertising of the camera manufacturer is designed to pull their products through the channel of distribution including camera stores, discount stores, mail order companies or any other type of middleman. The advertising campaign is supportive of all the advertising, catalogs, flyers, circulars and the other types of selling efforts that will be expended by retailers who carry the camera line.

The consumer advertising campaign by the manufacturer is indirect in that the reader of the advertisement cannot take immediate action and order the product from the advertiser. The reader must seek a source for the products, which would usually be a retailer who has an inventory of the product line. However, if the advertisements did solicit orders, the manufacturer in effect would become a direct marketer. An immediate negative reaction would come from all the camera retailers handling the products. The manufacturer would have become a competitor rather than being committed to "back retailers all the way." Without doubt, a good portion of the established channel of distribution would collapse. Few retailers would carry a line of cameras that was being sold direct to the ultimate consumer by the manufacturer.

The distinction between direct and indirect response advertising comes into focus when a manufacturer is willing to place general advertising in publications, while the ultimate consumer cannot order the product from the advertiser. The purpose of most indirect response advertising is to create or stimulate demand that results in the over-the-counter sales of the advertised product and to induce middlemen to handle and promote the advertised line. The middleman might be a catalog showroom, appliance dealer or any other type of retailer.

On the other hand, the promotional material or advertising of a catalog showroom can stimulate a combination of both direct and indirect responses on the part of the ultimate consumer. If a catalog showroom carries a number of cameras in advertising that has a direct response format—based on graphics, copy and order blank suggesting that the consumer order the products directly from the advertiser—then the catalog was designed to serve a direct response function. If the recipient of the catalog goes to the retail catalog showroom and picks up the camera advertised, the catalog has performed an indirect advertising function as far as the consumer is concerned. As a result, a catalog showroom often offers the consumer two choices: respond to the catalog advertisement directly and order the products by mail order for future delivery or respond indirectly by going to the showroom in person and purchasing the merchandise over-the-counter.

By definition, general advertising does not allow a direct response, and it is sometimes baffling to see full-page department store advertisements stating "no mail orders accepted." If the department store was capable of using direct response graphics, coupon and copy, the advertising would give the public the option of ordering by either mail or phone and in the process establish a mail order sales division. Most department stores offer only one option: for the consumer to visit the store and buy the advertised product, perhaps with the hope that they will purchase additional products on impulse.

In the example of the camera manufacturer, it might be assumed that there would be little need to offer drop shipping services since the manufacturer has a nationally advertised line of products and an established channel of distribution of middlemen who stock the products. However, most manufacturers have the marketing policy to utilize every available sales opportunity. By offering drop shipping services, the manufacturer may get large mail order firms or other direct marketers to promote the product line. These companies would not ordinarily handle the cameras unless drop shipping services were offered. In spite of the numerous advertising exposures financed by the camera manufacturer, nothing really happens until the product is finally sold to the ultimate consumer. Direct marketers, including a small, newly formed mail order company, can benefit from the massive general advertising campaigns of manufacturers by converting the stimulated demand in a presold market for the products into orders sold for future delivery, while the product source provides drop shipping services.

Few marketers can predict the exact quantity of a product that will be sold, based on a given amount of marketing or advertising. If it were possible to accurately anticipate the exact demand for products, the huge inventories of merchandise that fill the stockrooms and warehouses around the world might be reduced. On a more realistic level, a large mail order firm that produces 15 to 20 million catalogs a year might consider promoting the camera of a manufacturer who will provide drop shipping services as opposed to another camera producer who will not offer such services. If the manufacturer will not drop ship, the mail order firm is faced with the dilemma of deciding how much inventory should be stocked in anticipation of orders that will be generated by their own advertising or catalog promotions. The ideal inventory would be a quantity of cameras exactly equal to the total number of sales made, with no back orders, delays in shipment or left over, unsold merchandise. Drop shipping is one of the very few marketing functions that allows inventory requirements to equal demand, with the additional benefit that the products are purchased after the merchandise is sold to the ultimate consumer. Many major manufacturers provide drop shipping services as a means of offering middlemen an extra incentive to advertise and promote their products.

In the previous example, the camera manufacturer is spending a vast amount of money on general consumer advertising in an effort to create brand recognition and stimulate demand for products. Direct marketers, large or small, should consider promoting national brands on consumer electronics, sporting goods, appliances, housewares, clothing and the numerous other products that are heavily advertised by the manufacturer.

BENEFITS OF SELLING NATIONALLY KNOWN BRANDS

1. The public already has a favorable image of the products based on consumer awareness

2. General advertising by the manufacturer has to an extent presold the products to the public and stimulated demand, making it easier and less costly for middlemen to sell the products

3. Buyers are usually less hesitant to purchase a product by mail for future delivery when the product is produced by a large, major manufacturer who is already well known to the public

4. Major manufacturers offer product guarantees and warranties more often to assure the buying public of the quality of the products sold

5. Many nationally known products have a high price range that will afford a substantial gross profit on each sale, even if the product is discounted

6. Packaging of single units of the products, including proper cartons and protective materials used at the manufacturing level of major companies, are usually of excellent quality, assuring safe and undamaged shipment in single units

7. The seller can benefit from the millions of dollars' worth of sales promotion and advertising that has already been spent by the manufacturer in an effort to create demand for the products

8. Mail order advertising or direct mail can trigger an immediate response by offering to sell and ship merchandise, rather than requesting the consumer to appear at a local store to make a purchase

9. Nationally known brands of consumer goods are instantly recognizable by the public

10. The prestige, image and the quality of nationally known merchandise is a positive reflection on the seller

11. Through the use of drop shipping, the direct marketer can offer very competitive prices on national brands by eliminating the need for stocking inventory, along with other cost savings that are associated with the use of drop shipping as a marketing function

There are some potential disadvantages in selling national brands. They may be widely available in retail stores, and there may be little incentive for a consumer to buy by mail, unless the price is highly competitive. On the other hand, the consumer may be responding to advertising, based on the convenience of ordering a product by mail that is also available in a local store, even if the price is the same under both conditions. Many consumers will refer to various consumer reports to study product features of a camera, as an example, in addition to examining a specific model in a camera store. Once the potential consumer has decided to purchase a specific model of camera, the price of the product may be one of the major factors in making a decision to purchase the item in a retail store or from one of the many direct marketers that advertise in consumer camera magazines. The stock numbers and brand names of many cameras are so well known that many mail order firms only have to put the name of the manufacturer, the model and stock number and price in mail order advertising. An examination of any of the many consumer photography magazines will indicate many direct marketers selling cameras using model and price only, without the slightest description of product features.

PRODUCT COST EVALUATIONS

The cost determination of a product could be a science, while product pricing is an art. A manufacturer of a product or a middleman has to find out what a product costs and in some way determine how to price the product for resale. At the level of the manufacturer, the cost accountants can usually establish fairly accurate indications of the cost of a single unit of a product by adding up all the input costs of raw materials, labor, capital and overhead and dividing the total input costs by the number of units produced at various levels of production—up to the limits of the physical plant and equipment of the company. It is fairly obvious that unit costs of a product will usually go down as the volume produced increases.

The establishment of the price a manufacturer should charge a wholesaler, distributor or retailer is another matter. The markup could be a certain percentage of the cost of the product due to the lack of any other realistic method. If the cost to manufacture a product is $10, the producer could add on 100 percent of that cost factor to form a price of $20 per unit that would be charged to a wholesaler or retailer, depending on the channel of distribution. The manufacturer could arbitrarily decide to establish a unit price on sales to wholesalers of $19.50, $21 or $23 or some other price, subject to quantity discounts.

In addition to establishing the wholesale price of the product, the manufacturer may add on another 100 percent of the wholesale price to indicate a suggested retail price, even though the FTC does not approve of such a practice. There is nothing particularly scientific about applying 75 percent, 100 percent, 125 percent or more to the cost of a product to determine a wholesale or suggested retail price of an item. More than likely, these percentages are used because true costs are not available, and it may be customary to just add on a markup of 100 percent to costs.

Merchandise has subjective qualities that cannot be measured in terms of percentages. The eye appeal of a product may have a great deal to do with the pricing of an item. Other factors may include the price of competitive goods, demand elasticity, and the type of product. At the retail level, the basis for price determination starts with the unit price paid for the product, plus all overhead costs and hopefully a profit. Since overhead costs are difficult to determine for a single unit of merchandise, particularly at the retail level, a percentage markup on cost may be the usual method of determining the price. More often than not, the percentage markup results in a price similar to the suggested retail price, if indicated by the manufacturer. The final retail price is usually modified by markdowns or other competitive forces. The manufacturer has the additional problem of determining quantity discounts, based on the volume of purchases made by a wholesaler or retailer. The standard pack of the product sold to a wholesaler might be one dozen of the item at $240/doz., while an order for a gross might be offered at an additional 5 percent to 15 percent quantity discount. It is often difficult to prove that there is a specific cost savings in selling products in quantity that reduces the price by a fixed percentage or whether the quantity discounts are offered as an incentive for middlemen to purchase larger amounts of the product, regardless of any cost savings to the manufacturer.

PRODUCT COST AND PRICE DETERMINATION ON DROP SHIPMENTS

From the standpoint of both the supplier and user of drop shipping services, there is probably no other cost and price factor more important than that of a single unit of the product. If the manufacturer of the product can determine at what price they will sell a dozen of the item, there should be no particular problem in establishing a single-unit price. There are no doubt extra costs for the stocking entity in offering drop shipping services such as order handling and processing, along with shipping costs, if the product is offered on a delivered price basis. Accordingly, the single-unit drop ship price of a product is almost always higher than the single-unit price of the smallest quantity that is offered on a stocking basis. If a manufacturer will supply a wholesaler in a minimum quantity of one dozen of an item for $240 (unit price of $20 each), then the single-unit drop ship price would probably be $22 to $24 each or an amount that will defray the additional costs of processing drop shipped orders. The manufacturer may be offering drop shipping services to wholesalers or distributors as an accommodation for which extra charges are justified. The manufacturer, in that case, is retaining the marketing risks and costs associated with physical possession of inventory.

Once a stocking entity has determined the cost of providing a single-unit drop shipment, the question arises as to whether the exact cost of providing drop shipping services should be charged to the wholesaler or distributor or whether the drop shipper should mark up the cost to make an extra profit on the drop shipping services offered. For example, if a manufacturer can sell one unit of a product on a drop ship basis for $20 (not including shipping costs), there is already a built-in profit based on the $20 price. If the actual cost of drop shipping the product, including order handling, processing and record keeping is $3 per unit, it would appear that the single-unit drop ship price might be $23, plus shipping costs. However, this is a direct pass-through of costs, rather than profit-making on the drop shipping services as such. If a profit is to be made on the operation of a drop shipping department or function, then the single-unit drop ship price might be marked up to $25 to $26 per unit, as an example.

MAIL ORDER PRODUCT SELECTION BASED ON PRICE

Although there are still successful direct response products promoted that retail for $1.50—the sale of 1,000 envelope address labels, as an example—there has been a trend toward offering mail order products with substantially higher prices. It would appear to be difficult to make a profit selling 1,000 labels for $1.50, however one printer of such a product receives 40,000 orders a day and is, in fact, making a profit. Low-priced individual products offered through mail order advertisements in publications are often used as loss leaders for building a mailing list for bouncebacks or catalog follow-up with higher priced merchandise.

MEDIA COSTS AND DEMAND ELASTICITY
FOR PRODUCTS

Formats such as direct response ads in publications or through the creation of catalogs have fixed costs, regardless of the retail prices of the products advertised. A five-inch advertisement in a magazine may cost

$1,800, which is the same when offering a leather wallet for $5 or a $39 electronic clock. The advertisement for the wallet may generate ten times the number of orders than the ad for the clock and result in a greater profit. The retail price of mail order products has some relationship to the elasticity of demand. If 1,000 labels were advertised in the same space in the same publication at an assortment of prices: $1.50, $2.50, $4 or $5, there would no doubt be a marked drop in orders at the $5 price as the buying public might believe that this price was just too high for the product offered. Demand elasticity can be a measure of multiple orders. A mail order customer might order four pairs of pants from a direct marketer if they were $10 each, but if the same item sold for $15 each, the consumer might order only one, two or none at all. Mail order advertising is one of the few methods of testing product pricing, based on total response and profitability.

Many publications offer split-run editions under the condition that advertising copy, including the price of the product, can be changed halfway through the print production run. One million copies of a consumer magazine may carry an advertisement selling a product for $20 each by mail, and another million copies could indicate a price of $24.98 for the same product. Since the total advertising costs for each advertisement are identical, a comparison between the sales results at both prices can be made. Which advertisement produces the greatest net profit, based on the price of the item? That price should be used as a guide for pricing the product in future promotions. Other publications have regional issues that in effect offer the same testing possibilities as the split-run.

Advertising research studies usually indicate a very small percentage of readers of the total circulation of a major consumer magazine can recognize or even remember mail order advertisements based on recall tests. Due to the limited number of potential consumers that may even see a mail order advertisement in a publication, it would seem logical that an attempt should be made to sell higher priced products that may offer a better possibility of creating a profit.

There is also the factor of psychological elasticity of demand based on the price of different products. A mail order buyer may not hesitate to purchase a product for $5 by mail, but parting with $40 to $50 for an item might reduce potential sales, based on price alone, regardless of the features or merits of the product. Higher priced products can offer more flexibility in changing gross profits. An item might be offered originally at a price of $30 postage paid, for example. Results might indicate that the item would have to be increased in price to $37 to make a profit, based on projected sales at that price, from future advertisements. If an item that was selling for $5 and is increased in price by the same $7 amount, the new $12 cost to the consumer may drastically reduce the number of sales, since the item may only have the appearance of a $5 item.

There are numerous variables in the marketing mix of product, price and promotion with the eventual goal of profit. Marketing risks are incurred by every firm, and few can predict the profitability of a product promoted by mail order marketing methods. Testing various combinations of price, advertising media and promotion methods may be the only key to profitability. Perhaps the most useful guideline concerns the fact that higher priced products may be the best candidates for mail order promotion to offset ever-rising advertising costs.

8

Drop Shipping News

SOURCES FOR 90,000 DROP SHIPPED PRODUCTS

Drop Shipping News (P.O. Box 1361, New York, NY 10017) is one of the few publications devoted to the subject of drop shipping as a marketing function and the selling of products for future delivery through mail order and direct mail in particular. The publishers of *Drop Shipping News* also produce the *Drop Shipping Source Directory of Major Consumer Product Lines* that lists hundreds of manufacturers who drop ship single units of over 57,000 consumer products. In total, both publications developed research data on product sources that drop ship approximately 90,000 consumer products listed under these general classifications: appliances, automotive accessories, boats and marine equipment, books, clothing, craft and hobby kits, electronics (including TV, stereo, CB, recorders and calculators) floor coverings, furniture, garden equipment, giftware, hardware, health and beauty aids, health equipment, housewares, jewelry, luggage, office equipment, sporting goods, stationery, toys and novelties, watches and clocks and many other product lines.

The firms were compiled by contacting many thousands of consumer product manufacturers in the United States, all of which agreed in writing to be listed in the publications. Any directory is out-of-date to some extent the day it is published because the addresses of some firms change, and the mail forwarding period is in effect by the post office for only one year. It is difficult to trace the location of firms once they have moved. In addition, drop shipping is a marketing policy and, as such, is subject to change.

One manufacturer of full-sized sailboats in Florida had agreed to be listed in *Drop Shipping News* and to provide drop shipping services. Subscribers to the publication then stated that the sailboat manufacturer would not drop ship the boats. It was determined that a new sales manager had been appointed by this firm shortly after their listing appeared in *Drop Shipping News,* and the marketing policies of the firm were changed to discontinue drop shipping services entirely. Therefore, the search for firms that will agree to provide drop shipping services is a never-ending process. Many of the firms that offer drop shipping services provide nationally known brands, offer extensive product lines and are far from being small companies. To give an indication as to the vast number of products offered on a drop ship basis, a few of the listings that have appeared in past issues of *Drop Shipping News*, including descriptions of the products, follow.

TYPES OF DROP SHIPPED PRODUCTS
WITH DESCRIPTIONS

Single-unit drop shipping sources: (Supplier code: M-manufacturer, D-distributor, W-wholesaler, I-importer, followed by the number of items in the product line)

Archery (M–173)

American Archery Company now offers their line of bows, arrows and accessories on a single-unit drop ship basis, as well as in quantity. Their feature item is the Super Nitro compound bow, designed for fast, smooth action. The Super Nitro has a short length for use in heavy, wooded cover and allows fast aiming. Other bows include the Am-Mag fully laminated, high performance bow; the American Hunter, with bracket assembly and adjustable stable limb design; and the Cheeta I, target bow and the new Cheeta II, hunting bow, both with split limb, two-wheel compound and weight adjustment features. The firm also offers three models of Recurve Bows for schools and camps, along with two fiberglass models. Additional accessories include arrow rests, releases, tabs, covers, arm guards, quivers, bow cases, bow sights, arrow making supplies, target mats, stands and faces, along with bow strings and bow finishing equipment. This extensive line of archery equipment is outlined in an eight-page, four-color catalog. For full details, write: L.W. Armstrong, American Archery Co., P.O. Box 100, Oconto Falls, WI 54154.

Automotive (M–100)

Rite Autotronics Corp. of Los Angeles, California, offers a full line of products related to auto maintenance and tune-up. Their Model 9000

Dial-A-Pressure foot-powered air pump features micrometer pressure control, allowing the user to dial air pressure between 0 and 120 psi. The pump is easy to use and has adapters for use with car and bike tires, needle valve filled balls and cone valve filled rafts and toys. The supply source also produces a line of battery chargers that provide full rated output over the full charging period via solid state, electronic technology. Six models are offered: No. 8000, 4 amp battery charger; No. 8020, 6/2 amp battery charger; No. 810, 6 amp output at 6 and 12 volts; No. 8030, 6 amps at 12 volts; No. 8040 automatic circuitry, 10 amps at 12 volts; and 8050, 10 amps at 12 volts. All these units use 115–120 VAC. The test and tune-up equipment line is very impressive as indicated by the following products: Maxi-Tune Ignition Analyzer that performs fifteen basic professional tune-up tests, including idle and high RPM, point condition, dwell, idle and mixture, etc. The Volt-Ohm-Amp Tester offers complete electrical tests for all auto applications. The Dwell-Tach-Points tester analyzes these areas. A Universal Dwell-Points Tester is also offered, along with an Automotive Tune-Up Analyzer. The Model 1566, Automatic Diagnostic Analyzer offers many additional test capabilities. The supply source also offers a wide variety of gauges for in-dash mounting or in single, dual, or trio panel mounting kits, some of which are as follows: 270 degree GT tachometer; 270 degree Sidewinder Tachometer; Custom Speed Tachometer 0–8000 rpm; Electronic Tachometer; Torque Zone Indicator Tachometer; Torque Zone Tachometer and a 180 degree Electronic Tachometer. Many other lines are offered, including Continental Gauges, Astro Gauges and Sports Switches. The manufacturer will drop ship single units of this extensive line to the ultimate consumer, as well as in quantity for wholesalers. For full data, write; Henry S. Rose, Rite Autotronics Corporation, 3485 S. La Cienda Boulevard, Los Angeles, CA 90016.

Binoculars (MI–20)

Bushnell Optical Company, a division of Bausch & Lomb, is now offering a special binocular for the needs of the vacation traveler. The compact, hi-powered Vacation Binocular with a unique Kwik-Draw case is easy to carry and fun to use. As the binocular case is hung from the user's shoulder, a side panel access opening allows the user to withdraw the binocular for instant use. The model 13–8360, 8 × 30 Sportsview binocular, with Insta-Focus has a 394-foot field of view at 1,000 yards, exit pupil of 3.8mm, a height of 4–1/2 inches and weighs 18 ounces. The supply source will drop ship single units or in quantity for wholesalers. For data, contact: Carle F. Bode, Bushnell Optical Co., 2828 E. Foothill Boulevard, Pasadena, CA 91107.

Binoculars and telescopes (D–700)

Tasco Sales, Inc., of Miami, Florida, now offers a very extensive line of optics on a drop ship basis. The binocular line is described in a twenty-two-page, four-color catalog that features the new Bino/Cam, a two-in-one product that combines a quality 7-power, wide angle binocular and a compact 110 camera. Five models of Zip-Zoom binoculars feature one-finger focusing and zoom lever action. A similar group of six binoculars is available in twelve models, while European-styled models are offered in eight styles in an assortment of powers. Other binocular lines include International 300 binocular in six models; the Standard European Zip Focus binocular in five models; Standard European binoculars in six models; an economy series in four models; a promotional series; long-range American-style binoculars; rubber covered binoculars; roof prism binoculars; monoculars and theater models; sports and opera glasses. The range of powers in this line of binoculars includes 2.5×23mm, 4×30mm, $7–15 \times 35$mm, 7×35mm, $8–15 \times 50$mm, 12×80 mm, 16×50mm, 30×50mm, 20×60mm and many more. The features and other powers that are available are too numerous to mention. The Tasco microscope products include a line of kits with projector microscopes and science experiments and a student microscope with slide clips. Numerous additional accessories are available for microscopes and other items. Professional scopes include a 50x, 100x and 400x model, with stereo scopes of various powers in addition to a Bino-Professional model with interchangeable objectives. Tasco also offers a full series of magnifiers that include pocket sizes for jewelers and loupe models for watchmakers. Table top and a variety of hand-held magnifiers are also offered. The Tasco product line is extensive, and all items are of the highest quality. The supply source will drop ship single units of their products for direct marketers, as well as in quantity for wholesalers. For full details and drop shipping data, contact: Robert J. Johnson, Tasco Sales, Inc. 1075 NW Seventy-first Street, P.O. Box 380878, Miami, FL 33138.

Butcher blocks (M–90)

Brandenfels Blocks are handcrafts of Pacific Northwest red alder. This unique hardwood has a fine, uniform close grain and a very smooth texture. The honey-brown color offers the heirloom quality of all items within this beautiful and extensive product line. Counter top butcher blocks are offered in five sizes, along with portable kitchen islands, knife racks in five sizes, utility blocks in six sizes, hanging blocks in five sizes, grooved blocks in six sizes, blocks with legs in six styles and special variety sets that include an assortment of several items. The line of 17×29-inch end grain tables of the skirted type are available with either tapered legs, round legs or bakers tables with round or tapered legs. The beauty and quality of butcher block products can only be appreciated by physical examination. The manufacturer offers a twelve-page catalog showing these products in full color. The drop shipping program allows shipment direct to the ultimate consumer via UPS up to 100 pounds, and by motor freight over 100 pounds. The freight classification for cutting blocks is 24120, sub 5, class 55. For full details contact: Larry L. Nolder, HT Products, Inc., Brandenfels Blocks, Box 1108, Scappoose, OR 97056.

Camping equipment (M–100)

For over seventy-five years, The Coleman Company has produced camping and outdoor equipment of outstanding quality. Their product line is now available on a single-unit drop ship basis. The firm produces the unique Inflate-All 150, a portable air pump that works from any 12 volt automobile cigarette lighter outlet. Two air chuck adapters are included, along with a 13-1/2-foot power cord and a 3-foot air hose. The Inflate-All 150 can be used to pump up auto and bicycle tires, air shocks, rafts, boats and athletic equipment. The basic Coleman Outing Products line is extensive and includes the following items: Coleman lanterns including a Silk-Lite mantle that gives bright, even light, has a steel spout, screw-on cap, finger pump for air pressure and steady burning with a steel font that holds two pints of fuel. A total of five models are offered. Coleman stoves: Coleman stoves travel like a suitcase and cook like a kitchen range. Four models are available with various fuel and cooking capacities. The stoves feature a power pump fuel delivery, fuel tank cap, control valves, wind baffels, along with fully adjustable cooking power. Catalytic heaters: Coleman catalytic heaters give efficient, flameless warmth. A wick carries fuel to the heating pad, where a platinum catalyst burns fuel vapors without producing a flame. Coleman catalytic heaters are available in three models from 3500 to 8000 BTU capacities. Coleman sleeping bags: Every bag is machine washable, and the cover and liner material is preshrunk and color fast. Twelve models are offered with two weights of polyester filling material, with either cotton, nylon or nylon taffeta quilted outer covers. The linings are offered in flannel or cotton, while another complete line of twelve models has Dacron Holifil for filling and a variety of covers and linings. The complete sleeping bag line is colorful and of excellent quality. Coleman classic tents offer triangular windows, double seams, vinyl-coated nylon floors, nylon screens, inside zippers and a unique tent frame assembly system. The classic tents are available in four models that sleep from two to five persons. Other tent lines include two models of larger oasis tents, sleeping five to six people. Numerous other tents are available. For details, contact: John Criss, The Coleman Company, Inc., 250 N. St. Francis, Wichita, KS 67201.

Clocks (M–300)

The Howard Miller Clock Company produces a very large selection of wall-mounted, mantle and free-standing grandfather clocks that are depicted in several catalogs. The Howard Miller and Barwick Clock catalogs are in four colors and consist of fifty-six pages that describe over 100 styles of clocks that include collector's editions of the classic Regulator schoolroom styles, Dew Drop Calendar Clocks, Long Drop Regulator, American Railroad Regulator, The Welch Regulator, The Regency and the Jeweler's Regulator. Dozens of other mantle clocks are offered that are just too numerous to mention. A World Time Clock is in the form of a framed, five-color map of the world, indicating the time in seventy key cities throughout the world. Long-life fluorescent bulbs illuminate each time indicator window for easy reading. A full line of grandfather clocks are offered, each of which is registered and personalized by Howard Miller. Twenty ornate styles of grandfather clocks are offered and have retail prices up to $3,700. The movements of the clocks vary, depending on the model, but many include movements operated by battery, pendulum, key-wind, weight-driven pendulum and other drives and movements. A full line of modern clocks are depicted in another four-color, thirty-two-page catalog. An institutional line, includes many styles that can be mounted from the ceiling or wall for use in offices and other businesses. Dozens of other clocks are offered with suggested retail prices from $24 to $860, but most retail from $20 to $80. The manufacturer will drop ship single units, as well as in quantity. For full details, contact: Philip D. Miller, Howard Miller Clock Company, 860 E. Main Street, Zeeland, MI 49464.

Cutlery (MI–62)

The Washington Forge of Englishtown, New Jersey, has an extensive catalog program through which they drop ship single-unit sets of cutlery and flatware, in addition to drop shipping for wholesalers. The line is depicted in a twenty-four-page, full-color catalog which includes the Carriage House group of knife sets, housed in counter-top, butcher block style holders. The Deluxe Town and Country group of cutlery and hollow-ground steak knives are available in a hardwood holster, suitable for wall mounting. Twenty-nine different flatware settings are available that include a 23-karat electro gold-plated stainless tableware service for eight and other stainless steel place settings in a fifty-piece and seventy-four-piece service for twelve. For full drop shipping details, contact: Richard A. Warn, Director of Marketing, Washington Forge, Inc., 28 Harrison Avenue, Englishtown, NJ 07726.

Diamonds (M–264)

The Kohinoor Corporation will drop ship single units of their merchandise to the ultimate consumer for mail order firms and other retailers. The line includes a wide assortment of ladies diamond engagement rings and wedding bands, diamond cocktail rings, in addition to many styles of diamond rings for men, solid gold rings with onyx, topaz, pearls and birthstones, all of which are depicted in a sixteen-page, four-color catalog that is available on request. For details on their drop shipping program, contact: Werner Reiss, Executive Vice President, Kohinoor Corporation, 12th floor, City National Bank Building, Birmingham, AL 35203.

Folding furniture (M–41)

Metals Engineering Corporation of Greenville, Tennessee, offers a full line of products on a single-unit drop ship basis and in quantity for wholesalers. Their folding steel furniture includes metal chairs and matching folding bridge tables. The MECO chairs have stain resistant upholstery in vinyls, nylons and Herculons and have cushioned seats 1–1/2 inches thick for extra comfort. The chairs fold flat to a thickness of 3 inches and are fully guaranteed for ten years. All of the chair and table combinations are available in a wide variety of metal frames and upholstery colors. The chair and table sets are available in a Custom Series; the Royal Series, with extra thick seat cushions and back rests; the Imperial Series, that offers king-sized tables; and the Collector Series, with exclusive nylon upholstery. All of the chairs and tables are shown in a sixteen-page, four-color catalog. MECO also offers twenty-eight models of charcoal and gas barbeque grills of truly outstanding quality and appearance. The full line of grills is shown in a twenty-page, four-color catalog. For details on drop shipping, contact: Jan Menko, Metals Engineering Corp., P.O. Box 3305, Greenville, TN 37743.

Furniture, assembled (M–45)

Lu Van, Inc., offers a line of ready-to-assemble home furnishing that includes their model 5000 Mobil Bar, which is easy to assemble and is finished in walnut woodgrain, and the scratch and mar resistant top and sides give access to almost 15 inches of storage space. The unit retails for $96 and the firm produces forty-five other practical items that include shelving, storage cabinets, book cases and TV stands that are particularly adaptable to drop shipping since the products are packaged, ready for shipment by the manufacturer. For full details, contact: John J. Manion, Lu Van, Inc., 1129 S. Bridge Street, Belding, MI 48809.

Hand wrought iron (M–136)

The National Stove Works of Cobleskill, New York, forges a wide variety of wrought iron products under the Silent Steam Blacksmith brand. The brushed, tempered steel fry pans are preferred by many chefs, as hand forged steel is less porous than cast iron pans, allowing them to be used for cream sauces and quiches. The sizes of the forged steel pans are numerous, as well as the style of the handles and hanging racks. The product line includes many useful accessories for the home or kitchen and include bedside candle stands, flame tip andirons and dozens of other hand wrought items. Hearthside cooking sets are also available, along with special fireplace pan and wall brackets for fireplace tools. All of the items are hand made using the same techniques that blacksmiths have mastered through the ages using white hot iron, anvil and hammer. The products are described in a twelve-page catalog and price sheet. For full data and drop shipping details, contact: Sherri C. Deats, Sales Manager, National Stove Works, Inc., Silent Steam Blacksmith, P.O. Box 649, Cobleskill, NY 12043.

Lawn equipment (M–35)

The Lambert Corporation offers an outstanding line of quality lawn and garden equipment. The manufacturer produces the largest line of lawn sweepers available on the market today. The sweepers are offered in numerous styles, some of which are the push type that can hold up to 10 bushels. The Lambert lawn sweepers are rugged, as they can pick up litter, twigs, grass, leaves and small stones. The units can be converted to trailer sweepers. Many of the heavy-duty lawn sweepers have a "flipomatic" feature allowing rear dumping. All of the fourteen models of the sweepers have numerous features and options including a Thatch 'N Sweep attachment that pulls down lawn clippings. The manufacturer also produces the Lambert Broadcast Spreader, Select-A-Flow spreader, Golden Harvest electric cultivator, High Wheel Cultivator, with 24-inch diameter steel wheels and many other types of related products. The company offers this top quality line on a single-unit drop ship basis, as well as in quantity for wholesalers. For full details and color catalog, contact: Harold D. Johnson, Vice President Sales, Lambert Corporation, 519 Hunder Avenue, Dayton, OH 45404.

Leather goods (M–600)

Action Leathercraft, a manufacturer of over 600 items, will drop ship single units of their products to the ultimate consumer for dealers. Their newest item, the BC–1 California Latigo briefcase is made from genuine

California Latigo leather. The case is handcrafted, and it comes with antique locks and hardware. The natural distinguishing marks of the branding iron guarantee the first quality of top grain leather. The extensive products offered by this manufacturer are too numerous to mention. For full details on drop shipping, contact: Cathy Burgess, Special Accounts, Action Leathercraft, Inc., 5340 E. Harbor Street, Commerce, CA 90040.

Leather luggage (M–85)

Leather remains the leader in denoting quality in luggage. The Carter-Wall Corporation manufactures a very attractive line of eleven styles of leather attache cases with brass hardware, many with combination locks. Portfolios are offered in six styles, tennis and men's bags in six styles, and a wide assortment of luggage is available in sizes up to 26 × 19 × 11 inches, along with flight bags and pilots' cases. The firm produces a top quality line of products with suggested retail prices of up to $165. For full details and catalog covering drop shipping, contact: Sidney Peterson, Carter-Wall Corporation, 33 N. La Salle Street, Chicago, IL 60602.

Lighting systems (M–150)

The Audio-Carpenter Division of Walter Kidde & Co. offers their complete line of emergency lighting equipment, portable lights and electronic megaphones on a single-unit drop ship basis as well as in quantity. The emergency lighting units are for use in an office, store or home and automatically turn on during a power failure. Each of the fifteen models is wall or bracket mounted and has flood/spot lampheads designed especially for emergency lighting by providing maximum illumination. Also available is a full line of self-powered emergency exit lights, all of which are UL, OSHA, National Electrical Code and Life Safety coded. Over thirty models of electronic megaphones are offered that include a personal PA system using a 9 volt battery, a professional electronic megaphone with a 4 watt capacity, a larger model using four standard 9 volt batteries and an 8 watt megaphone with a built-in signal alert. Each of three product lines is described in a four-color catalog. For data on their drop shipping program, contact: L. D. Armentrout, Audio-Carpenter Division, Walter Kidde & Co., Inc., 706 Forrest Street, Charlottesville, VA 22901.

Lucite products (M–100)

AKKO, Inc., of Andover, Massachusetts, manufactures a variety of lucite items for home and office. Most items are in crystal clear acrylic, with a selected group in Tortoise Acrylic. Personalization with the engraved names or initials is available on many items, such as trays, napkin holders, eyeglass caddy, clipboards, letter holders and other items. The firm also produces a large number of planters and other home horticulture accessories such as brackets and swivel ceiling books. The firm can supply many items for business and industry with their logo or other personalization for customers. The firm offers single-unit drop shipping services, as well as drop shipments in quantity for wholesalers. For details, write: Daniel Frishman, AKKO, Inc., Dundee Park, Andover, MA 01810.

Luggage—attaches (M–34)

Baltimore Luggage Company offers the Amelia Earhart line of luggage for women and is available in matched sets. All products are made from scuff-proof grained vinyl, with contoured handles, die cast chrome locks, patented T-frame closure, quilted interiors, full-strap hinges, and all items are individually boxed in factory-fresh cartons, ready for shipment. The full line consists of numerous styles of 21-, 24-, 27-, and 30-inch luggage in addition to attache cases, ladies' carry-on bags, tote bags, overseas bags two-suiters, dress bags and a large 40 × 24 suit bag. The manufacturer also offers the Stripes line of bags with die cast combination locks. The 24-inch Junior Pullman, 27-inch Pullman and the 30-inch Overseas Dress Bag are available with wheels, pull rings or chain leashes. The luggage is of outstanding quality. For full details on drop shipping contact: Joseph A. Rivkin, The Baltimore Luggage Company, 304 N. Smallwood Street, Baltimore, MD 21223.

Mailboxes (M–30)

Spear Engineering Company offers a complete line of custom inscribed markers and nameplates on a single-unit drop ship basis. Their Day-N-Night custom marker shines in lights at night and identifies a home to callers, day or night. The marker is custom embossed on solid aluminum plates and their 18 × 2-1/2 inch size can accommodate up to seventeen, 1–1/2-inch high letters and numbers that are white-reflector beaded and headlight bright. The mailbox marker line is offered in seven styles, along with five styles for use as lawn markers and five styles for use on a post. Each marker includes scrolls and a rustproof, aluminum frame. Other styles of markers include those made of different materials and finishes. All orders are shipped within forty-eight hours on a drop ship basis. For details, contact: John W. Spear, Spear Engineering Company, 3107 N. Stone, P.O. Box 7025, Colorado Springs, CO 80933.

Musical instruments (MI–500)

Musical instruments at popular prices and of all types are offered on a drop ship basis by the Stradolin Corporation. Sales can be made to schools or individuals and include guitars, harmonicas, drums, violins—in fact, all types of musical instruments for a total of over 500 products. Attractive catalog material, as well as photos and sales literature, are available from the supply source. For drop shipping details, contact: Lee Saltzman, Stradolin Corporation, 370 Motor Parkway, Hauppague, NY 11787.

Office accessories (M–200)

America's oldest manufacturer of desk accessories offers their line of products on a single-unit drop ship basis to the ultimate consumer, as well as in quantity for wholesalers. The desk sets include numerous styles with matched desk pads, ashtrays, calendar pads, memo holders, double pen bases, pencil cups and in-out trays with or without covers. The Flair 5100 series is in brass, while the 5500 series is in bronze. The Jen Risom line combines oiled walnut and soft, supple leathers, while the 900 series consists of hand oil-rubbed solid oak. Other desk accessory lines are in matched leather and walnut and combinations of cowhide or naugahyde. This product line is truly of outstanding quality, backed by eighty-three years of skilled experience. The items are described in a fourteen-page, four-color catalog. For drop shipping details, contact: Paul Sainberg, Sainberg & Co., 18 W. Eighteenth Street, New York, NY 10011.

Office signs (M–1,000)

Safety Advisors Manufacturing offers an unusual drop shipping plan for firms that sell to other businesses. The firm produces six basic lines of vinyl and acrylic signs that include over 1,000 stock items, too numerous to list. The firm has the capability of producing signs to custom order. OSHA now requires many more safety and directional signs in both office and factory. All of the signs produced by Safety Advisors comply with OSHA specifications, local fire codes and military requirements. Their high-impact plastic signs do not break, bend or scratch. The company offers full drop shipping services on single or multiple units, with price markups that usually exceed 100 percent. All orders are shipped the same day from an inventory of over 340,000 stock signs that are on hand at all times. The firm provides sales kits, artwork, layouts, glossy photos, color transparencies and other aids for advertising production. For full drop shipping data, contact: Jay Gilbert, National Sales Manager, Safety Advisors, 64 Old Orchard Road, Skokie, IL 60076.

Photographic equipment (M–100)

The Chinon Company has been producing fine cameras and stereo systems for over thirty years and is the world's largest manufacturer of movie cameras. Their vast product line is produced in eleven plants throughout the world. The Chinon Corporation of America in Springfield, New Jersey, is the domestic marketing and distribution arm of Chinon in the United States. The products include the Auto-Magic Super–8 Sound Camera; Automatic CE–3 Memotron and Semi-Automatic CM–3; 35mm SLR cameras that will accept the new Chinon Power Plus Winder; the 35F-A, 35 Compact Auto-Focusing and 35F–35; Automatic Compact, with built-in flash; the Chinon 60AF XL, Super–8 sound camera; Chinon Pacific 80SMR and 60SMR XL; Super–8 sound movie camera with laps dissolves; the DS–300 sound projector; Chinon Pacific 200/8XO, 8 to 1 Super–8 sound camera, with 200-foot film capacity; the Budget Chinon 7800 projector, along with a very extensive line of 110 cameras, 35mm cameras and lenses. The technical data on this extensive line could fill thirty typewritten pages. For many years Chinon made the lens parts for Canon and other leading Japanese photo industry manufacturers. Chinon accounts for more than one third of Japan's total exports of 8mm movie cameras. With corporate headquarters in Tokyo, Chinon's production facilities are centered in Suwa City, some 200 miles northwest of Tokyo, in the foothills of the Japanese Alps. Chinon was a pioneer in beginning production in the local pristine air, which is ideal for the manufacture of high-tolance, precision instruments. Since then, the city has attracted many high-precision manufacturers, earning the area the nickname of the "Switzerland of Japan." The manufacturer will drop ship single units of their products, as well as in quantity for wholesalers. For full details, contact: Glenn Heckendorf, Chinon Corporation of America, Inc., 43 Fadem Road, Springfield, NJ 07081.

Photographic products (M–80)

Hanimex (U.S.A.) offers a complete line of photographic merchandise on a single-unit drop ship basis only. The products include the Hanimex line of pocket cameras, with accessories; 35mm SLR cameras in five models, many with power zoom along with a full line of tripods, light meters and viewers. The manufacturer will also drop ship single units of eight models of pocket calculators, from a basic unit to a super scientific model with eight-digit display and AC adapters. For data, contact: Richard Z. Cox, Hanimex (U.S.A.), 1801 Touhy Avenue, Elk Grove Village, IL 60007.

Radios (MI–75)

Heritage International offers a line of radios that are concealed within small boats, dolls and replicas of famous cars. The firm also distributes battery-operated telephone number finders, extension telephones, music boxes, casino games for home use, desk clocks and three-dimensional picture clocks. The firm will drop ship single-and multiple-unit orders. For full details, contact: Jack Auster, Heritage International, 1280 North Avenue, Plainfield, NJ 07062.

Sporting goods (M–100)

Spaulding, the famous manufacturer of sporting goods, offers an impressive line of equipment on a single-unit drop ship basis for mail order firms. These products are grouped into six, four-color catalog sheets. Golf includes items such as KroFlite Gold Balls, Era I Woods, Era I Irons, Era I Sand Clubs, Futura Men's eleven-piece Golf Set, Futura Ladies' eleven-piece Golf Set, Lady Spaulding eleven-piece Golf Set, Epic 2000 Men's eleven-piece Golf Set, Era I Golf Balls, Tee Flite Men's R.H. Golf Set and the Tee Flite Ladies' R.H. Golf Set. The Tennis catalog includes the Official Table Tennis Set, Impact 500 WCT Tennis Racket, Champ ED Yellow Tennis Balls, along with a Squash Racket, Carry-All Bag, Badminton Doubles Set, Racquetballs, and Tennis Gift sets. Their Game catalog offers many types of tennis rackets, softball gloves, tournament table tennis sets, badminton doubles sets, footballs, soccer balls and volleyballs. Other products that are available include their Futura Racquetball Racquet, Ace Golf Balls, WC Australian Tennis Balls, JSV Leather Football, Top Flight eighteen-panel Volleyball, Tournament Soccer ball and many other items. The worldwide recognition of Spaulding sporting goods adds value to a line that is of excellent quality. For full details on their single-unit drop shipping program, contact: William E. Barry, Spaulding, 7 Killmer Road, Edison, NJ 08817.

Stoves (W–96)

This product line includes four models of an old-fashioned cookstove. The Victor, Jr., wood-coal range was originally designed in 1911 and is made for heat, hot water and cooking, while adding to the decor of a den or living room. The oven is cast iron, with replaceable firebox liner. The Victor, Jr., is an antique style stove, with castings that have weight and thickness to take the high temperatures generated by coal. The stove weighs over 300 pounds, is shipped via motor freight and has a suggested retail price of $600. Also available is a large number of dual energy oil and electric lamps, including chandeliers. The solid brass lamps are replicas of those made during the gold rush. The product source will drop ship single units for dealers. For details, contact: K. P. Silver, Pioneer Lamps & Stoves, 71 Yesler Way, Seattle, WA 98104.

Telephones (M–500)

Saxton Products offers hundreds of telephones and electronic hardware, including the following items: decorator telephones, hardware kits, aerial kits, alignment tools, amplifiers, antenna hardware, buzzers, cables, CB and HAM accessories, coils, connectors, controls, cord sets, TV couplers, demagnetizers, earphones, guy wire, headphones, hookup wire, intercom sets, jacks, knobs, lamps, meters, microphones, plugs, potentiometers, printed circuit boards, radio accessories, recording accessories, relays, resistors, sockets, speakers, splicers, stereo accessories, switches, terminals, transformers and numerous other items which are described in a fifty-three-page catalog. The source is a prime manufacturer of the products which are produced in three plants located in the United States. The firm will drop ship single units of all of the items in their catalog, as well as in quantity for their wholesalers. For full data, contact: Louis Gould, Saxton Products, Inc., 215 N. Route 303, Congers, NY 10920.

Television sets (M–50)

The full line of General Electric TV sets is available on a single-unit drop ship basis and includes black-and-white models with 12-, 15- and 19-inch diagonal screens. All have the General Electric energy saver chassis and are 100 percent solid state, cool running integrated circuits. The color television line includes models with 10-, 13-, 17-, 19-inch screens and others with a full 25-inch diagonal screen. The 25-inch color table and console models include the new modular, 100 percent solid state chassis, in-line picture tube system, black matrix tube for brilliant color. For details on the GE-TV line, including drop ship data, contact: Frank Berlucchi, General Electric Company, TV Business Department, Portsmouth, VA 23705.

Thermometers (DI–80)

The Abbeon Company offers a line of products for boat owners, campers and sportsmen, as well as for home and industrial use. The products include accu-art rulers, altimeters, auto altimeters, barographs, barometers, ship's barometers, ship's clocks, clinometers, compasses, drafting templates, epoxy putty, hygrographs, contact hygrometers, container hygrometers, dip shaft hygrometers, hygrostats, linen testers, multidraft instruments, plastic sheets, psycrometers, sling plycrometers, sauna instruments, surgical scalpels, photo tachometers, thermometers of various types, water activity analyzers and weather stations. The products can be sold through a twenty-four-page catalog that can be imprinted with the name of the dealer on the front cover, and all of the products are available on a single-unit basis, with discounts of 30 percent to 50 percent of the prices listed in the catalog. For full drop shipping data, contact: Martin R. Carbone, Abbeon California, Inc., 123 Gray Avenue, Santa Barbara, CA 93101.

Thermos bottles (M–109)

Okay Industries provides a single-unit drop shipping program on their full line of Thermosware. Vacuum bottles are offered with a standard neck, seamless glass vacuum bottles and high-impact plastic outer case. Rubber shock absorbers and cushioned gaskets provide maximum protection for the glass. Other products include insulated mugs, thermos bottles with full grip handles, wide mouth vacuum bottles, children's lunch kits, executive beverage servers in chrome or walnut grained finishes, and numerous other items for camping. For drop shipping data, contact: Frederick W. Voos, Okay Industries, Inc., Vacuum Products Division, 3580 Main Street, Hartford, CT 06120.

VAST NUMBER OF DROP SHIPPED PRODUCTS

The examples of the products and sources mentioned in this chapter indicate that a wide variety of items are available on a drop ship basis. The literature from manufacturers and distributors who have been listed in past issues of *Drop Shipping News* would more than fill a five-drawer filing cabinet. There are thousands of other firms that provide drop shipping services and offer tens of thousands of products. Although most of the product sources indicated in the previous sections produce consumer products, a large number of manufacturers and distributors of industrial products also provide drop shipping services. The entire function of drop shipping can be applied equally to both consumer and industrial products, although this book has centered on consumer products and mail order product promotion, since all merchandise is sold for future delivery—the main criteria for the use of drop shipping as a marketing function. The means for gaining up-to-date information on product sources that provide drop shipping services is outlined in greater detail in the following chapter.

DROP SHIPPERS SEARCH FOR DEALERS

Manufacturers and distributors of both consumer and industrial products usually sell through middlemen who are contacted through personal selling, direct mail, telemarketing or advertising in trade publications. For the most part, there are publications that are distributed to middlemen who market every conceivable type of product. Likewise, there are mailing lists of mail order catalog companies, mail order houses, discount stores, department stores, specialty shops and numerous other types of retailers, in addition to wholesalers, distributors, dealers and jobbers of both consumer and industrial products. It is acknowledged that most manufacturers and stocking distributors prefer to sell to middlemen who stock inventory of the products sold, but many of these same supply sources will also provide drop shipping services. The offer to drop ship products is usually contained in the wholesale product literature of the manufacturer or distributor or openly promoted in trade publications. Following is a copy of a letter from a listee in *Drop Shipping News* indicating interest in gaining dealers who would utilize the drop shipping services offered by the supply source:

Artistic Greetings, Inc.
409 William Street
Elmira, NY 14901

Mr. Nicholas T. Scheel
Editor, *Drop Shipping News*
P.O. Box 1361
New York, NY 10017

Dear Mr. Scheel:
   Belatedly, we wish to express our appreciation for including information on our personalized stationery Mini-Catalog Program in your February issue.

   We were extremely pleased with the increase in inquiries since the information appeared in your publication. While it is difficult to determine sources for all inquiries received, we do know that at least ten in the past two weeks were the result of your article. (These ten faithful *DSN* readers specifically mentioned your publication in their requests.)

   As editor, you may sometime wonder whether your words are read. From the inquiries received, we can tell you they are. We will keep "tracking" responses and give you an up-date in a couple of weeks.

   Once again, thank you for including information on our products in your fine publication. We would sincerely appreciate any mention you can give in future editions.

Sincerely,

Aloysius F. Stanton
Sales Manager

9

Drop Shipping Sources

FOREIGN DROP SHIPPERS

Numerous importers stock merchandise and provide single- or multiple-unit drop shipping services for dealers. The drop shipping services provided by importers who stock merchandise are no different from services provided by drop shippers who stock products made in the United States. A substantial number of manufacturers in foreign countries will drop ship single units of products direct from an overseas location to the retail customers of domestic U.S. mail order firms. These manufacturers can be found by contacting the trade missions of various countries or from trade directories of foreign manufacturers, arranged by product groups or the country of origin.

For a membership fee, a few firms will provide source information regarding foreign drop shippers who can supply consumer products at very low prices that may be suitable for mail order promotion, as compared to the same type of product that could be produced in the United States. In spite of the low prices that may be offered by manufacturers in foreign countries, the bulk of all such products are unbranded novelties, toys, gadgets or decorative handcrafted items, often produced by cottage industries or in factories where the workers are paid very low wages. There is no doubt that many of the products available from manufacturers in foreign countries can be successfully and profitably promoted by U.S. dealers by the use of the drop shipping services provided by overseas product sources. However, there are potential problems that any dealer in the United States should consider before getting involved with foreign drop shipments. The reliability of the product source in a foreign country may be questionable, since there may be a time lapse of many months between gaining product information and samples and placing advertisements for the product in publications or catalogs. In the interim, the foreign manufacturer may have discontinued the product or changed the color or specifications, which may create massive delays in drop shipping orders, in the event that the supply source runs out of inventory. Product availability on a continuing basis may be a special problem when dealing with foreign manufacturers, since it would be difficult to enforce any agreement regarding standardization of products, prompt fulfillment of orders or any other failure in performing drop shipping services.

In other cases, the volatile exchange rates of U.S. dollars and the currency of the country in which the drop shipper is located may also pose difficulties. As an example, the U.S. dollar has fallen 50 percent in value against the Japanese yen from 1983 to 1988 which would affect product costs. Prompt shipment of drop shipped orders may create another problem for U.S. dealers, since the FTC does not appear to make any distinction between domestic mail order and foreign order fulfillment under the 30 Day Mail Order Rule. It is hard to envision that a retail consumer could order a product from a mail order dealer in the U.S. and expect 30-day delivery, if the order is forwarded to a manufacturer in India for drop shipment. If the dealer in the U.S. cannot ship within thirty days or if the order cannot be filled within a reasonable length of time, every customer of the dealer would have to be notified of any delays to conform with the FTC 30 Day Mail Order Rule.

Other problems that the dealer may encounter regarding drop shippers in foreign countries concerns the potentially large volume of paperwork that may be required: documentation, letters of credit and the possible need for converting U.S. dollars into foreign currency. If there are delays regarding drop shipments, the use of international FAX or telephone may be required, in addition to foreign airmail letters and perhaps a foreign language requirement. Product liability insurance may not be carried by manufacturers of products made in foreign countries. Even if such insurance were in force, how could a retail consumer make a product liability claim against a manufacturer located in India, or some other country?

The governmental agencies that are responsible for product safety are particularly concerned with the design and fabrication of children's toys made overseas. Government inspectors have been known to seize bulk shipments of toys as they enter the United States because knobs, beads, handles or parts may be easily broken off the toy and cause children to choke. If a consumer can prove that a child was injured or died based on a hazardous product made by an unknown manufacturer in a foreign country, the U.S. importer or dealer may end up as a defendant in a liability claim case.

Many foreign countries do not have stringent regulations on the materials from which products are manufactured. Domestic firms are required to adhere to stricter regulations regarding flammability of nightgowns, dresses, curtains and other products made of fiber. There have also been cases where the lead content of paint on toys or decorative material may be dangerous, in addition to high lead content in pottery and ceramics. A consumer may order a set of coffee mugs made in a foreign country. The lead might leach into the coffee, and, over a period of time, the user is slowly poisoned. Large importers, distributors or even retailers may have access to an import buying service that thoroughly tests products made in foreign countries, or they may have their own testing laboratories. Small firms may not be able to afford proper product testing to determine the contents or safety of imported products.

Most of the potential difficulties that may arise by having products drop shipped by manufacturers in foreign countries concern the types and quality of the products and the reliability of the source. Of course, a dealer may have similar problems with domestic firms that drop ship single units. But dealing with drop shippers in foreign countries may amplify any problems that might develop because of the time lapse in communications, differences in language and currency, along with product safety, standardization, quality and availability. Consumer electronics such as VCR units, TV sets or cameras that are produced by large manufacturers in Japan, as an example, are usually of excellent quality. However, the majority of these overseas manufacturers of consumer electronics will not drop ship single-unit orders direct to the customers of dealers in the United States. The bulk of such products exported by manufacturers in Japan are shipped to the offices of their own companies located in the United States. Some of the distribution centers owned by foreign manufacturers will drop ship from inventory held in this country. The majority of foreign manufacturers that maintain inventory of products in this country will only sell in quantity to stocking distributors who may in turn drop ship single-unit orders for appliance, consumer electronics or camera retailers or for mail order firms.

In addition to directories of foreign manufacturers and sources provided by trade missions, there are numerous mailing lists of overseas manufacturers, based on the types of products produced or the country of origin. International trade publications may also carry display or classified advertising listing foreign manufacturers who are seeking importers in the United States. Firms interested in importing products can also place advertising in such publications and specifically request responses from manufacturers that will drop ship. Numerous books and publications cover the subject of importing and product sources overseas.

IMPORTERS PROVIDING DROP SHIPPING SERVICES

Numerous firms import virtually every type of product, drawing upon the resources of manufacturers worldwide. The independent importer usually deals in a related group of products and, in the process, determine product quality standards, the reliability of the manufacturers, and merchandising insight as to whether the product can be sold profitably in the United States. An importer will not knowingly import a product that cannot be sold. Once an independent importer has physical possession of inventory, they have the option of selling to other middlemen who stock merchandise, or they may provide drop shipping services for middlemen in single- or multiple-unit quantities.

Many retailers or mail order firms may prefer to deal with full-function importers who stock merchandise rather than getting involved in direct importing. Since the cost of imported products may be low, compared to similar products made in the United States, the stocking importer can usually offer competitive prices to dealers. The profit margin made by the importer reflects the "value added" to the product, based on the function of product selection in addition to taking physical possession of inventory. Whether the importer will provide drop shipping services is a marketing policy decision that is identical to that of any domestic manufacturer or distributor who stocks inventory.

A "pure" full-function importer only stocks products made in foreign countries. However, an importer of sporting goods may also stock sporting goods made in the United States. The ratio of the percentage of products that are imported, relative to the quantity made in the United States may vary from one firm to another. Most marketing authorities use the 50 percent rule in defining marketing functions. If over half of the products stocked are imported, the distributor is an importer and, by stocking inventory, can perform the same drop shipping services as a manufacturer or wholesaler. Drop ship orders are initiated by middlemen. The orders in turn are forwarded to the importer who stocks the merchandise and ships the product to the customers of the middlemen. In this transaction, the importer is the drop shipper.

In a slight variation of the function of drop shipping, the importer could receive an order for a quantity of a product from a middleman, but rather than ship from inventory held by the importer, the order could be sent to a manufacturer in a foreign country that would drop ship the products direct to the customer of the importer in the United States. In this transaction, the importer is initiating the drop ship order, while the foreign manufacturer is in fact the drop shipper.

MANUFACTURERS PROVIDING DROP
SHIPPING SERVICES

The manufacturers of both consumer and industrial products have perhaps the largest centralized inventory of their products and are in an excellent position to provide drop shipping services for distributors, wholesalers, jobbers and retailers. In addition, the manufacturer can make key decisions as to the type of packaging in single units that would be most adaptable for shipment by parcel post, United Parcel Service or motor freight. A manufacturer who packages individual units of products in mailable corrugated cartons is providing packaging that is perhaps best suited for single-unit drop shipments. It may be easier for a manufacturer to establish a special department to handle drop shipment in single units, as compared to the drop shipping facilities of stocking distributors or wholesalers. A specific quantity of inventory could be packaged in single units and transferred to the drop shipping department, while the balance of the products manufactured could be packaged and stored for shipment to middlemen who stock the product in quantity.

Middlemen who initiate drop ship orders will usually attempt to contact the manufacturer of the product when negotiating with drop shipping sources of supply. Middlemen who use the drop shipping services of a manufacturer can usually be assured of a stable source of supply, with relatively little risk that the manufacturer will be unable to fill drop ship orders promptly. In addition, the manufacturer may be able to offer the lowest single-unit drop ship price as compared to the drop ship price of single units at the distributor or wholesaler level. Lower drop ship prices provided by the manufacturer may be based on lower operating and overhead costs. The storage or warehouse costs incurred by the manufacturer would no doubt be lower than the storage facilities of a middleman. Manufacturers are usually located in geographic areas designated for industrial production where the cost per square foot of storage space could be considerably less than warehouse costs of middlemen who may be closer to or in high-rent urban centers.

If a prime manufacturer will not drop ship single units of products, middlemen may be forced to contact the next level in the channel of distribution, which is usually a stocking distributor who may provide drop shipping services, or possibly a stocking wholesaler. However, each succeeding level in the channel of distribution that has physical possession of products must include the cumulative costs of inventory, associated marketing risks, and a profit to determine a drop ship price to be charged to middlemen who initiate drop ship orders. The single-unit drop ship price of a product increases as additional functional middlemen intercede between the manufacturer and the firm seeking drop shipping product sources. Therefore, most middlemen would prefer to utilize the drop shipping services of the manufacturer of the product in an effort to obtain the lowest drop shipped price and a reliable source of supply. Manufacturers may also offer many types of advertising and promotion materials to middlemen who initiate drop ship orders.

DISTRIBUTORS PROVIDING DROP SHIPPING SERVICES

A distributor is usually a full-function middleman who stocks merchandise purchased directly from manufacturers. Distributors are also the first classification of middleman in a multilevel channel of distribution. The product line of distributors may be restricted to a specific group of related products such as sporting goods, air conditioners, appliances, consumer electronics or, in the case of industrial distributors, such product lines as equipment, machinery, tools, lubricants, abrasives or various types of raw materials. The prices of products sold by manufacturers to this classification of middleman can be defined as "distributor prices," which are often based on large car or truckload quantities of products.

Depending on the size of the distributor and the large inventories of merchandise usually held in stock, the distributor is in a position to sell to wholesalers who in turn sell to retailers or industrial end users. Many manufacturers will not sell directly to wholesalers or retailers and require that all orders for their products be purchased from their distributors that stock inventory. The manufacturer is in effect protecting the business interests of the network of regional distributors, since the business relationship between the manufacturer and distributor may be jeopardized if the manufacturer bypasses the distributors by selling direct to wholesalers or retailers.

A distributor who stocks inventory has the marketing policy option of providing drop shipping services for wholesalers or, under less frequent circumstances, for retailers or mail order firms. If the distributor has a policy of selling direct to very large retailers, department stores or mail order firms, the distributor may drop ship single units of products to the ultimate retail consumer. As an example, a large furniture distributor may sell to a department store that is unwilling to stock furniture that duplicates an inventory already held by the distributor. The stocking distributor of furniture could drop ship single units of the product line direct to the retail customer of the department store. Although the department store may have to pay the distributor for providing drop shipping services, the store does not have to pay for the furniture until after it is sold, nor do they have to incur the costs of stocking the product. The wholesaler who might be positioned in the marketplace between the distributor and the department store has been eliminated from the channel of distribution.

The furniture distributor may also have a drop shipping arrangement with various furniture manufacturers. The distributor who usually stocks inventory of the products may also initiate drop ship orders. If there is a large order of furniture from a retailer that the distributor does not stock, the distributor could send the order direct to the furniture manufacturer who would drop ship the order direct to the retailer. In rare occasions the manufacturer might even drop ship direct to the retail customer of the department store.

WHOLESALERS PROVIDING DROP SHIPPING SERVICES

Wholesalers usually carry a wider selection of related products, as compared to a distributor. A sporting goods distributor may stock large quantities of the line of products of three to ten manufacturers, while a wholesaler may purchase and stock inventory of dozens of distributors and hundreds of manufacturers. Wholesalers may act as a type of local warehouse for retailers who can gain fast delivery of inventory from the wholesaler, covering a variety of products.

From the standpoint of drop shipping, a wholesaler can initiate drop ship orders that are sent to either a distributor or manufacturer who in turn will drop ship products to a retailer or business end user. In addition, a wholesaler can act as a drop shipper by accepting orders for multiple- or single-unit quantities of products from retailers (including mail order firms) and drop ship direct to the ultimate consumer. The decision as to whether a wholesaler will deal in drop shipments is the same type of marketing policy decision that is made by a distributor.

Retailers usually order products in quantity and are supplied directly from inventory held by the wholesaler or manufacturer. Retailers may also purchase direct from distributors, if there is no wholesaler positioned as a middleman between the distributor and retailer. Wholesalers who initiate drop ship orders usually involve dozen or gross lots, unbroken cartons, factory-sealed containers or other standard units as supplied by the manufacturer or held in inventory by distributors.

Wholesalers who stock inventory may provide drop shipping services for retailers or mail order firms in single-unit quantities of various products. Mail order firms seeking a source for single-unit drop shipments will usually prefer to have the manufacturer of the product perform drop shipping services to gain better prices and to be assured of a large, stable inventory source. If a manufacturer will not drop ship in single units, a mail order firm or retailer may have to rely on a distributor or wholesaler to perform this service. The prices paid by retailers for products drop shipped by wholesalers contain the cumulative costs and profits of the manufacturer, distributor (if any) and the wholesaler.

RETAILERS INITIATING DROP SHIP ORDERS

Retailers and mail order firms have two options: They can stock inventory purchased from manufacturers, distributors, importers, wholesalers or other middlemen, or they can initiate drop ship orders. The advantages and disadvantages of the use of drop shipping as a marketing policy by middlemen have been mentioned, and many of these same factors apply to retailers who initiate drop ship orders. Since the single-unit drop shipment of the products is related to mail order retailing in particular, an earlier section of this book has been devoted to drop shipping and the sale of products for future delivery by mail order firms through direct response advertising in publications, direct mail and catalogs.

COMPILERS OF MAILING LISTS OF MANUFACTURERS

Middlemen including retailers, mail order firms, wholesalers and distributors are constantly seeking new products and product sources, in addition to locating manufacturers or stocking entities who will provide drop shipping services. The names and addresses of specific groups of manufacturers are not difficult to acquire, based on the availability of a large number of business directories, data from trade associations and other sources for the tens of thousands of producers of both consumer and industrial products. The most comprehensive source for information on mailing list compilers, brokers and managers is contained in *Direct Mail List Rates and Data*, Standard Rate and Data Service, Inc., 3004 Glenview Road, Wilmette, IL 60691, and copies of this publication are usually available in the business section of public libraries.

Some of the consumer product mailing lists available include manufacturers under the general classifications of appliances, books, ceramic china and glassware, bicycles, giftware, decorative accessories, furniture, golf, hardware, housewares, home furnishings, jewelry, garden equipment, luggage and leather goods, musical instruments, notions, office equipment and stationery, photography, sporting goods, toys, hobbies and novelties and many more. Industrial product manufacturers are available in mailing list formats and include such product groups as air conditioning, automotive supplies, brushes, electrical products, farm implements, lighting, metal working, paint, paper, plastics, plumbing, stone products and dozens of other types of products.

Middlemen who are seeking product sources may find it cost effective to rent mailing lists of manufacturers, rather than to compile their own lists. On the other hand, rented mailing lists may not be as up-to-date as lists compiled from other sources such as trade publication directories. The obvious purpose for rented mailing lists is to contact potential supply sources by the most effective method. Mailing lists for the most part are used for generating address labels. The usual mailing list format for the names and addresses of the companies is on pressure-sensitive or Cheshire labels. Mailing lists are usually available arranged in alphabetical order by states, in alphabetical order by name of company or person or in zip code sequence. The rental cost for compiled mailing lists can run from $25 per thousand names and addresses to as high as $75 per thousand for very specialized lists.

As an example, list compilers have mailing lists of consumer product manufacturers. One such firm, Consolidated Marketing Services, Inc. (P.O. Box 1361, New York, NY 10017) offers lists on pressure-sensitive mailing labels. Other list compilers and brokers offer similar mailing lists. Following is a sample group of mailing lists of manufacturers, available from Consolidated Marketing Services, indicating the general product group, the types of products manufactured and the approximate number of companies within each product classification.

Appliances, electronics and housewares—3,000 firms

Air conditioners	Hi-fi equipment
Air purifiers	Home computers
Audio components	Kitchen items
Barbeque grills	Personal items
Calculators	Plastic items
Car radios	Power tools
CB radios	Radios, scanners
Clocks	Refrigerators
Cookware	Security alarms
Cutlery	Smoke detectors
Dishwashers	Stereo systems
Dryers	Tableware
Electric ranges	Tape recorders
Electronic games	Telephone accessories
Fans	Telephones
Floor care	TV sets
Freezers	Typewriters
Gas stoves	Video cameras
Grills	Video recorders
Heaters	Washers

Crafts and Craft supplies—1,200 firms

Adhesives	Clay
Applique	Cord
Beads	Crochet
Bells	Cross stitch
Boxes	Decoupage
Brushes	Doll houses
Buttons	Dolls
Candles	Easels
Canvas	Eggery
Cement	Embroidery
Ceramics	Etching

Felt
Frames
Glass
Hardware
Jewels
Knives
Leather
Macrame
Miniatures
Molds
Needlecrafts

Paper
Quilting
Rugmaking
Scissors
String art
Tape
Tools
Transfers
Weaving
Woodcraft
Yarn

Giftware—2,000 firms

Acrylic gifts
Alabaster
Albums
Antiques
Art decor
Ashtrays
Baby gifts
Bags
Banks
Barometers
Bars
Baskets
Bath, boudoir
Beer steins
Bells
Bookends
Boutique
Bowls
Boxes
Brass, bronze
Candles
Canisters
Carving sets
Chimese

Clocks
Collectibles
Cookware
Crystal
Dinnerware
Figurines
Fireplaces
Furniture
Glassware
Gourmet items
Lamps
Men's gifts
Paper goods
Pewter
Plaques
Pottery
Sculpture
Silverware
Souvenirs
Stoneware
Toys
Trivets
Wall decor
Woodenware

Housewares—1,700 firms

Air purifiers
Bar accessories
Baskets
Bathroom items
Brushes

Candles
Can openers
Carpet care
Chemicals
Choppers

Chromeware
Cleaners
Clocks
Closet accessories
Clothes dryers
Condiment sets
Cookware
Cutlery
Decoratives
Dinette sets
Dinnerware
Drapes
Enamelware
Fans
Fireplaces
Floor care
Garden items
Glassware
Hardware
Heaters
Home security
Ironware
Kitchen accessories
Ladders
Laundry aids
Mats, pads
Microwave
Mirrors
Paints
Paper goods
Personal care
Pet accessories
Planters
Plasticware
Stainlessware
Storage units
Table covers
Wire goods

Luggage and leather goods—500 firms

Address books
Albums
Attache cases
Back packs
Bags
Bars
Belts
Billfolds
Briefcases
Bruch kits
Camera cases
Clocks
Commercial Cases
Compacts
Desk accessories
Envelopes
Eyeglass cases
File cases
Fitted cases
Games
Garment bags
Handbags
Hat boxes
Identification tags
Jewel boxes
Key cases
Laundry bags
Lighters
Luggage, men's
Luggage, women's
Manicure sets
Money belts
Money clips
Padlocks
Photo frames
Portfolios
Purses
Ring binders
School bags
Sewing kits
Tie cases
Tool cases
Trunks
Trunks, steamer
Umbrellas
Valets
Watch straps
Wig cases

Musical instruments—1,300 firms

Accessories	Harpsichords
Accordions	Mandolins
Amplifiers	Microphones
Autoharps	Mirimbas
Bagpipes	Music stands
Baritone horns	Oboes
Bassoons	PA systems
Bugles	Pianos
Chimes	Piccolos
Clarinets	Pickups
Cornets	Saxophones
Cymbals	Speakers
Drums	Synthesizers
English horns	Trumpets
Guitars	Violins
Harmonicas	Xylophones

Office supplies, stationery—2,600 firms

Addressing items	Filing cabinets
Artists items	Fountain pens
Ball-point pens	Index cards
Billing equipment	Labels
Binders	Loose leaf
Bookkeeping supplies	Luggage
Brief bags	Mailing equipment
Cabinets	Markers
Calculators	Office furniture
Carbon paper	Paper
Cash registers	Pencils
Chairs	Plaques
Check writers	Postal scales
Coin sorters	Printing equipment
Copiers	Projectors
Data processing	Recorders
Daters	Rubber Stamps
Desks	Safes
Desk sets	Stationery
Dictating equipment	Tablets
Drafting equipment	Telephones
Duplicators	Time recorders
Embossers	Tyhpewriters
File folders	Visual aids

Photographic equipment, cameras—750 firms

Adaptors
Agitators
Alarms
Analyzers
Backs
Bellows
Binoculars
Cameras, movie
Cameras, still
Cameras, 35 mm
Chemicals
Close ups
Copiers
Darkrooms
Dryers
Easels
Enlargers
Envelopes
Film, movie
Film, sheet
Film, 33mm
Frames
Heaters
Lamps

Lenses
Lights
Loaders
Magazines
Masks
Meters
Movie equipment
Photo paper
Processors
Projectors
Reels
Reflectors
Safelights
Screens
Spotlights
Tanks
Telescopes
Testers
Timers
Trays
Tripods
Video equipment
Viewers
Washers

Tableware and accesories—500 firms

Bar accessories
Candle holders
Carving sets
Ceramics
Chinaware
Crystal
Earthenware
Figurines
Glassware

Mugs
Pewter
Pitchers
Plasticware
Silver flatware
Silver plate
Stainless steel
Stoneware
Tumblers

Video software—700 firms

Beta, VHS recorded video
Blank videotape cassettes
Home computer software
Video cassette cabinets

Video games and discs
Video movies, all subjects
Video software packages
Video storage systems

CONSUMER PRODUCT TRADE PUBLICATIONS

Whether middlemen are seeking domestically produced products for the purpose of stocking inventory or to search out firms that will provide drop shipping services, the most timely and accurate source information can be found in trade publications. Almost every consumer product group falls under a classification covered in depth by a trade magazine. These publications can offer an insight into consumer trends in addition to keeping readers informed as to new products. If a middleman plans to specialize in the marketing of housewares, consumer electronics or sporting goods, a subscription to the trade magazines that are devoted to these product groups is an excellent investment.

In addition, the publishers of a sporting goods magazine, as an example, may produce a separate yearly directory of all of the manufacturers, major distributors and importers of sporting goods in the United States. Other trade magazines may produce the same type of directory information as the thirteenth issue of a yearly subscription to the magazine.

Probably the most accurate source for information on trade publications is contained in *Business Publications Rates and Data*, published by Standard Rate and Data Service, Inc., 3004 Glenview Road, Wilmette, IL 60091. In addition, extensive listings of business publications can be found in other directories that are usually available in public libraries. Look for *The Standard Periodical Directory*, published by Oxbridge Communications, Inc., 150 Fifth Avenue, New York, NY 10011, which lists over 60,000 publications under 250 subject areas. Oxbridge Communications also publishes the *National Directory of Magazines*, which can be a source for publications covering specialized industries, markets or product groups. Here are a number of trade publications by product group classifications.

Appliances

Consumer Electronic & Appliance
  News
3821 W. 226th Street
Torrance, CA 90505

Dealerscope Merchandising
401 N. Broad Street
Philadelphia, PA 19108

(Also publishers of *Who's Who
  Industry Directory of Manufacturers
  and Distributors, Consumer
  Electronics and Major Appliances*)

Arts

Art Material Trade News
6255 Barfield Road
Atlanta, GA 30328

Crafts Report
700 Orange Street
Wilmington, DE 19801

International Art Material
Directory and Buyers Guide
6255 Barfield Road
Atlanta, GA 30328

Automotive Accessories

Aftermarket Business
120 W. Second Street
Duluth, MN 55802

Auto Merchandising News
234 Greenfield Street
Fairfield, CT 06430

Automotive Aftermarket News
65 E. Wacker Place
Chicago, Il 60601

Automotive Marketing
Chilton Way
Radnor, PA 19089
(Including Automotive Marketing
Retail Aftermarket Guide)

Automotive Products Report
7300 N. Cicero Avenue
Lincolnwood, IL 60646

Jobber and Warehouse Executive
950 Lee Street
Des Plaines, IL 60016

Jobber Retailer
110 N. Miller Road
Akron, OH 44313

Modern Tire Dealer
110 N. Miller Road
Akron, OH 44313

China and Dinnerware

China, Glass & Tableware
1115 Clifton Avenue
Clifton, NJ 07013
(Including China, Glass & Tableware
Red Book Directory Issue)

Clothing and Accessories

Accessories
50 Day Street
Norwalk, CT 06854

Apparel Merchandising
425 Park Avenue
New York, NY 10022

Hoisery and Underweare
120 W. Second Street
Duluth, MN 55802

Women's Wear Daily
7 East 12th Street
New York, NY 10003

Furniture and Accessories

Accessory Merchandising
408 Olive Street
St. Louis, MO 63102

Casual Living
370 Lexington Avenue
New York, NY 10017

CompetitivEdge
305 W. High Street
High Point, NC 27260

Furniture World
200 S. Main Street
High Point, NC 27261

Home Furnishings Review
110 World Trade Center
Dallas, TX 75258

Professional Furniture Merchant
180 Allen Road, NE
Atlanta, GA 30328

Unfinished Furniture Industry
1850 Oak Street
Northfield, IL 60093

Garden Supplies

Garden Supply Retailer
12400 Whitewater Drive
Minnetonka, MN 55343

Lawn and Garden Marketing
9221 Quivira Road
Shawnee, KS 66215

Outdoor Power Equipment
1904 Wenneca
Ft. Worth, TX 76101

Giftware

Accessories Today
200 S. Main Street
High Point, NC 27261

Accessory Merchandising
408 Olive Street
St. Louis, MO 63102

Art Business News Buyer's Guide
60 Ridgeway Plaza
Stamford, CT 06905

Catalog Product News
911 Hope Street
Stamford, CT 06907

Decor Sources
408 Olive Street
St. Louis, MO 63102

Gift and Stationery Business
1515 Broadway
New York, NY 10036

Gift Digest
170 World Trade Center
Dallas, TX 75258

Gift and Decorative Accessories
51 Madison Avenue
New York, NY 10010

Giftware News
350 Fifth Avenue
New York, NY 10118

Greetings Magazine
309 Fifth Avenue
New York, NY10016

Souvenir
1414 Merchandise Mart
Chicago, IL 60654

Souvenirs & Novelties
7000 Terminal Square
Upper Darby, PA 19082

Golf

Golf Industry
1450 NE 123rd Street
North Miami, FL 33161

Golf Pro Merchandiser
7 East 12th Street
New York, NY 10003

Golf Shop Operations
5520 Park Avenue
Trumbull, CT 06611

Hardware

Do-It-Yourself Retailing
770 N. High School Road
Indianapolis, IN 46214

Hardware Age
Chilton Way
Radnor, PA 19089

Hardware Merchandiser
7300 N. Cicero Avenue
Lincolnwood, IL 60646

Hardware Trade
2965 Broadmoor Valley Road
Colorado Springs, CO 80906

Housewares

Department Store News
425 Park Avenue
New York, NY 10022

Discount Merchandiser
215 Lexington Avenue
New York, NY 10016

Entree
825 7th Avenue
New York, NY 10019

Housewares
120 W. Second Street
Duluth, MN 55802

Import–Export

Global Trade
401 N. Broad Street
Philadelphia, PA 19108

Journal of Commerce Import Bulletin
110 Wall Street
New York, NY 10005

Interior Design

Interior Design Buyers Guide
249 West 17th Street
New York, NY 10011

Interior Design Handbook
370 Lexington Avenue
New York, NY 10017

Sweet's Catalog File
1221 Avenue of the Americas
New York, NY 10020

Luggage and Leather Goods

Showcase
350 Fifth Avenue
New York, NY 10118

Travelware
50 Day Street
South Norwalk, CT 06854

Musical Instruments

Musical Merchandise Review
100 Wells Avenue
Newton, MA 02159

Music Trades Magazine
80 West Street
Englewood, NJ 07631

Music and Sound Retailer
25 Willowdale Avenue
Port Washington, NY 11050

Photographic Products

Photo Business
1515 Broadway
New York, NY 10036

Photographic Trade News
210 Crossways Park Drive
Woodbury, NY 11797

Sporting Goods

Action Sports Retailer
P.O. Box 348
South Laguna, CA 92677

Fishing Tackle Retailer
1 Bell Road
Montgomery, AL 36117

Active Wear Business Magazine
13402 N. Scottsdale Road
Scottsdale, AZ 85254

Fishing Tackle Trade News
P.O. Box 2669
Vancouver, WA 98668

American Firearms Industry
2801 E. Oakland Park Blvd.
Ft. Lauderdale, FL 33306

Outdoor Retailer
31652 2nd Avenue
South Laguna, CA 92677

Archery Business
319 Barry Avenue South
Wayzata, MN 55319

Outside Business
1165 N. Clark Street
Chicago, IL 60610

Army-Navy Store & Outdoor Merchandise
567 Morris Avenue
Elizabeth, NJ 07208

Saltwater Dealer
1 Bell Road
Montgomery, AL 36117

Bowling and Billiard Buying Guide
101 E. Erie
Chicago, IL 60611

Shooting Sports Retailer
142 Ferry Road
Old Saybrook, CT 06475

Ski Business
573 Post Road
Darien, CT 06820

Skiing Trade News
1515 Broadway
New York, NY 10036

Sporting Goods Business
1515 Broadway
New York, NY 10036

Sporting Goods Dealer
1212 N. Lindbergh Boulevard
St. Louis, MO 63132

Sports Trend
180 Allen Road
Atlanta, GA 30328

Sports Style
7 East 12th Street
New York, NY 10003

Tennis Buyers Guide
5520 Park Avenue
Trumbull, CT 06611

Tennis Industry
1450 NE 123rd Road
No. Miami, FL 33161

Wear Magazine
P.O. Box 740995
Dallas, TX 75374

Television and Video

Autosound and Communications
345 Park Avenue South
New York, NY 10010

Consumer Electronics
345 Park Avenue South
New York, NY 10010

Dealerscope Merchandising
401 N. Broad Street
Philadelphia, PA 19108

Official Video Directory
P.O. Box 2740
Palm Springs, CA 92263

Retailer News
249 E. Emerson Avenue
Orange, CA 92665

Twice
902 Broadway
New York, NY 10010

Video Business
345 Park Avenue South
New York, NY 10010

Video Store
1700 E. Dyer Road
Santa Ana, CA 92705

Toys, Crafts, and Hobbies

Craft and Needlework Age
225 Gordons Corner Road
Manalapan, NJ 07726

Craftrends
6405 Atlantic Boulevard
Norcross, GA 30091

Creative Products News
P.O. Box 584
Lake Forest, IL 60045

Profitable Craft Merchandising
P.O. Box 1790
Peoria, IL 61656

Hobby Merchandiser
225 Gordons Corner Road
Manalapan, NJ 07726

Sew Business
15400 Knoll Trail Drive
Dallas, TX 75248

Miniatures Dealer
1027 North 7th Street
Milwaukee, WI 53233

Toy & Hobby World
345 Park Avenue South
New York, NY 10010

Playthings
51 Madison Avenue
New York, NY 10010

Trim-A-Tree Business
345 Park Avenue South
New York, NY 10010

Books

Some of the most prestigious, multimillion-dollar book publishers provide drop shipping services for dealers, covering many titles and readership interests. In addition, many will offer to supply mail order firms and trade magazine publishers with fully prepared advertisements which can be reproduced in a publication, catalog or as direct mail. The prepared ads, photos, veloxes and other promotion material are usually supplied without charge to dealers. The only investment on the part of the dealer or publisher is to run the ad in a magazine or to reprint the material. When orders are received for books, the dealer prepares a shipping label, which is sent to the "special order" department of the book publisher, which in turn drop ships the book to the customer of the dealer. Because the bookkeeping systems of large book publishers are geared to monthly billing on drop shipped orders, the dealer gets the benefit of drop shipping services in addition to having credit extended on such orders. Trade discounts on drop shipped orders are usually 33 percent to 40 percent off list, plus shipping costs.

One of the most accurate sources for data on book publishers is *Literary Market Place—The Directory of the American Book Publishing Industry* by R. R. Bowker Company. This directory contains the names and addresses of all major book publishers, the year founded, the number of titles currently published, total number of books in print and the names of sales and marketing executives. A source for books produced by self-publishers is the American Bookdealers Exchange (P.O. Box 2525, La Mesa, CA 92041) through their publication *Book Dealers World*. This firm also publishes the *Book Dealers Dropship Directory* which offers source data on over 1,000 books available on a single-title drop ship basis at 50 percent discount off the suggested retail price of the book.

INDUSTRIAL PRODUCT DROP SHIPPING SOURCES

Middlemen who are seeking suppliers that will drop ship industrial products, equipment or materials no doubt have already determined the product line they plan to promote. There is a vast array of different industrial product groups, and most middlemen specialize in a specific type of product distribution. Letters of inquiry to industrial product manufacturers can be similar to those suggested earlier for consumer product manufacturers. The basic information requested by middlemen would include product literature, pricing information and whether the industrial product manufacturer will drop ship products. Inquiry letters can more specifically define the types of products being sought by the middleman, and the potential source of supply could be informed as to the types of products currently sold by the middleman. If an industrial product manufacturer will in fact drop ship products, and the middleman wishes to promote the items, then the manufacturer can be asked to supply photos, graphics and additional product information, along with the details regarding the handling of drop shipping transactions, shipping cost factors and credit terms.

MAILING LISTS OF INDUSTRIAL PRODUCT SOURCES

As with consumer products, mailing lists of manufacturers for virtually every type of industrial product are available. The middleman who specializes in the sale or distribution of adhesives, sealants, tapes, lubricants, cutting tools or any of the tens of thousands of other types of industrial products can obtain mailing lists of these specialized groups of suppliers from mailing list brokers or compilers on a rental basis. The most complete reference for specialized mailing lists of industrial product manufacturers is contained in the *Direct Mail List Rates and Data* published by Standard Rate and Data Service, Inc., 3004 Glenview Road, Wilmette, IL 60691. Within this publication are listings of broker/compilers who specialize in the mailing lists of industrial product manufacturers by Standard Industrial Classification. Mailing lists of industrial product manufacturers usually rent for $50 to $75 per thousand names and addresses, supplied on pressure-sensitive mailing labels.

TRADE ASSOCIATIONS AND DIRECTORIES

Industrial product manufacturers are often members of trade associations that produce industry publications and directories of members. Due to the vast number of membership groups, a valuable reference would include the *Encyclopedia of Associations* published by Gale Research, Inc., Book Tower, Detroit MI 48226. It lists comprehensive data on over 25,000 national and international associations. The directory *Trade and Professional*

Associations of the U.S.A. (1350 New York Avenue, Washington, DC 20005) lists over 6,000 domestic trade associations. Because the manufacturers of industrial products may be listed in very specialized directories, a comprehensive source would include the *Directory of Directories*, published by Gale Research, that contains 2,000 pages and lists 10,000 business directories. Its international section includes trade directories covering Africa, Central America, Eastern Europe, Western Europe, Far East, Middle East, North America, Oceana, South America and the West Indies and is divided into specific industry groups.

There are also directories of manufacturers for virtually every state in the United States. These state directories are very detailed, covering a wide variety of manufacturers of every conceivable type of product. For middlemen who are seeking drop shipping sources of regionally produced or heavy products, state directories of manufacturers may be of great value. Perhaps the largest directory of manufacturers in the United States is the *Thomas Register of American Manufacturers* and the *Thomas Register Catalog File*, published by the Thomas Publishing Company, 1 Penn Plaza, New York, NY 10001, that lists virtually every type of industrial product manufacturer in this country. This massive, multivolume directory can be invaluable to middlemen who are seeking drop shipping sources.

On the international level, the U.S. trade missions of many foreign countries can offer a vast amount of information regarding foreign manufacturers who are seeking importers in the United States. Many of these industrial product manufacturers will drop ship direct to the customers of middlemen, particularly in the area of expensive, bulky machinery or printing presses, as an example. Middlemen can write directly to the manufacturers in foreign countries requesting product literature, pricing information and drop shipping data. The trade missions of foreign countries may also offer middlemen free services such as supplying mailing lists or directories of manufacturers in addition to acting as a link between U.S. importers and companies within specific foreign countries. Trade missions may also provide data on commercial directories—as examples, the *Korean Directory*, published by the Korean Directory Company, C.P.O. Box 3955, Seoul, Korea, is a massive 1,700-page publication that lists 5,000 manufacturers in Korea; and the *Japan Yellow Pages*, 6–9 Lidabashi 4-Chome, Chiyoda-Ku, Tokyo 102, Japan, which contains listings of 28,000 Japanese companies.

INDUSTRIAL PRODUCT TRADE PUBLICATIONS

Industrial trade publications provide valuable information on product sources. As cited earlier for consumer products and just as important for industrial product sources, the most complete and accurate guide for information on trade publications is contained in *Business Publications Rates and Data*, published by Standard Rate and Data Service, Inc., 3004 Glenview Road, Wilmette, IL 60091. Oxbridge Communications, Inc., 150 Fifth Avenue, New York, NY 10011, publishes two directories that can provide information on industrial product trade magazines: *The Standard Periodical Directory*, listing over 60,000 publications under 250 subject areas, and the *National Directory of Magazines*. If a middleman has a specialty of distributing a specific group of industrial products, a publication no doubt relates to the manufacturing of those products. Industrial product trade magazines can be invaluable to middlemen. They can supply the knowledge of new products, processes or materials and lead to product source information.

As in the case of consumer trade publications, industrial magazines often publish a directory of manufacturers, major distributors and importers of a specific type of industrial product, and a subscription to the publication related to the interest of middlemen is a necessity.

USE OF RENTED MAILING LISTS OR DIRECTORIES

Middlemen seeking product sources have the option of renting a mailing list of a specific group of manufacturers from a list broker or compiling their own mailing list through the use of directories. If the product line sought by the middleman may be produced by only fifteen to twenty manufacturers, the mailing list of these companies may not be available through a mailing list broker or commercial compiler. If there are compiled lists available on a rental basis for a small number of specialized manufacturers, the commercial compiler no doubt has used a directory that is available to the middleman. If a specialized list of manufacturers only contains twenty-five to seventy-five firms, the compiler could charge $50 to $75 for the list, even if it contained only twenty-five firms. As an example, a list containing the names of eighty-nine furniture pad firms would cost the minimum list rental price of $75. Middlemen seeking product sources that drop ship would find more accurate information by compiling their own mailing list from trade directories. Renting mailing lists from compilers or brokers becomes cost effective when the number of manufacturers is large. As an example, a mailing list of 5,737 furniture manufacturers can be rented from a list compiler for $50 per thousand names or for a total cost of $286.85. A middleman seeking furniture manufacturers that will drop ship would no doubt find that renting the mailing list would be far less expensive than compiling a mailing list from trade directories.

THE CONTINUING SEARCH FOR DROP SHIPPERS

A limited number of directories are available that list firms known to drop ship either consumer or industrial products. Drop shipping is a marketing policy that is subject to change. A new marketing management group that has never offered drop shipping services may at any given time agree to provide drop shipping services or to discontinue such services as the case may be. It is also a known fact that a relatively small percentage of all manufacturers or full-function distributors will drop ship products. There is no accurate way of determining how many of the over 5,000 furniture manufacturers in the United States will drop ship single units of their furniture product line. As a result, continuous research is required by middlemen in the form of letters of inquiry to search out manufacturers or distributors who will drop ship either consumer or industrial products.

10

Costs and Marketing Risks of Inventory

INVENTORY REQUIREMENTS OF MANUFACTURERS AND RETAILERS

There are probably only two types of businesses where the possession of inventory is inescapable. A consumer product manufacturer combines raw materials or parts with labor, management and capital to eventually produce an inventory of finished goods. It is estimated that, in total, U.S. manufacturers hold over $100 billion in inventory at any given time. At the other end of the distribution channel, a grocery store, department store or retailer of products sold over-the-counter must maintain an inventory to supply merchandise to customers at the time of sale. Middlemen—including distributors, jobbers and wholesalers—have the option of either stocking inventories of all products sold to the next level in the distribution channel or having drop shipping services provided by a stocking entity that is usually a manufacturer or another middleman.

A manufacturer who sells only to full-function middlemen that stock inventory has shifted physical possession of finished goods to the next level in the distribution channel, which can be spread geographically across the country in warehouses, storerooms or on the shelves of a variety of types of middlemen. The manufacturer of the product may continually ship quantities of inventory from a warehouse that may contain only 20,000 square feet, but the storage space allocated by middlemen to accommodate the product within the channel of distribution may be over 400,000 square feet. By selling to full-function middlemen, the manufacturer is filling the channel of distribution with inventory. The total cumulative costs of inventory maintenance are eventually included in the price paid for the product by the ultimate consumer or end user. As products flow closer to the ultimate consumer, as in the case of a retail store, the space allocated for individual products is usually small, compared to the space allocated for maintaining an inventory of the product at the manufacturing or distributor level. The cost of space at the retail level however may be relatively high when compared to the warehouse costs at the manufacturing level. A manufacturer may rent storage space for $10 per square foot; a middleman may pay $20 per square foot; and a retailer may pay $75 per square foot to store the same quantity of the same product, in addition to incurring all of the other costs and risks of inventory maintenance.

COST OF MAINTAINING INVENTORY
BY MANUFACTURERS

Perhaps the largest single inventory of any given product is in the possession of the manufacturer. The production planning by the manufacturer should include the continuous utilization of plant, equipment, capital and personnel to produce inventory in anticipation of sales. There are many books on the subject of production planning, plant utilization, scheduling, incremental expansion of production capacity and such books should be reviewed. However, the cost factors surrounding finished goods inventories, ready for sale to middlemen, are the areas that have a relationship to the marketing policy of a manufacturer who offers drop shipping services. If a manufacturer does not provide drop shipping services, the product may emerge from the production line in a factory-sealed carton, to be placed in another multiunit carton, ready for shipment in quantity to middlemen. If the manufacturer does provide drop shipping services from finished goods inventory in single units, additional space may be needed to process such orders, along with the requirement for additional personnel to fill single-unit or small orders.

COST OF MAINTAINING INVENTORY BY MIDDLEMEN

At every level in the channel of distribution, the same types of inventory costs are present. The amount of labor and storage space may vary, but middlemen have the same types of inventory maintenance costs as those of manufacturers. As products flow from the manufacturer to the distributor, wholesaler and retailer, the cumulative cost of inventory can be a key factor affecting profits. In total, the dollar value of inventories held by all middlemen is many times greater than the inventories of manufacturers. The "value added" to the price of merchandise through the function of inventory maintenance adds billions of dollars to the cost of products purchased by the ultimate consumer. These costs are incurred to have the right product, at the right time, at the right place to complete the over-the-counter sale to the ultimate consumer. The buying public pays a tremendous amount of money for the privilege of gaining the immediate transfer of physical possession of goods at the time of sale.

INVENTORY MAINTENANCE COSTS

The costs of maintaining inventory can be viewed from several perspectives: the determination of costs and risks of inventory maintenance, the shifting of part of those risks to others, or eliminating inventory maintenance entirely. From the standpoint of drop shipping, the entity that provides drop shipping services must have inventory whether the drop shipper is the manufacturer or stocking distributor. The middleman who initiates drop ship orders, on the other hand, does not directly incur the fixed or variable costs of inventory maintenance because that function is retained by the business entity that currently has physical possession of the products and has agreed to provide drop shipping services. From another point of view, the middleman who initiates drop ship orders has shifted the direct costs of inventory maintenance backward through the channel of distribution to the stocking entity.

To varying degrees, some of the costs relative to the storage and maintenance of inventory are discussed in the following sections.

FINANCIAL COSTS OF PURCHASING INVENTORY

Inventory represents a capital investment that cannot be realized until the inventory is sold. The sources of capital necessary to purchase inventory may be financed from continuing business operations, retained profit or by borrowing from banks or other sources. Manufacturers and middlemen alike can delay temporarily the costs of inventory by taking advantage of sales terms offered by suppliers in the form of payment arrangements such as 2/10 N30 or net thirty. The day of reckoning is short-lived in that the cost of purchasing inventory must usually be paid within thirty days. There are incremental costs of inventory that relate to the quantity of products purchased, all of which must be financed. Financial considerations may involve the concept of "the alternate uses of capital" under which money spent on inventory might have been more productively invested in other business operations. However, as long as a business entity stocks inventory of products, there is no escaping the direct costs of financing the purchase of inventory or providing capital for that purpose.

STORAGE COSTS

Storage costs to house inventory include land, buildings, warehouses, stockrooms and loading platforms or counter or display space in retail stores. The cost of any facility to store inventory may be financed from current operations or by borrowing from financial institutions. The storage area may be in a building owned by the business or rented from others. In either case, storage costs are usually fixed. A warehouse of 200,000 square feet carries the same financial costs whether the building is only 10 percent filled with inventory or whether it is filled to capacity. The dimensions of such inventory storage space are constant, as are most of the costs. The inflexibility of storage space costs translates into variable overhead costs. If only 10 percent of storage space for inventory is used, then all of the costs of the space are allocated to the sales value of the inventory at a 10 percent space utilization level. If the storage space is filled to capacity, the total cost of storage is spread over a larger inventory base. The rigidity of existing space for inventory storage is complicated by the fact that warehouse and storage facilities are never continually utilized at any particular level of capacity such as 10 percent, 50 percent, 85 percent or 100 percent. From a cost accounting standpoint, the overhead costs of inventory storage are constantly changing. Accordingly, inventory storage costs allocated to each individual unit of product is difficult to determine and may complicate the establishment of the wholesale or drop shipped price of the products sold.

STORAGE SYSTEMS AND EQUIPMENT

In addition to the costs of storage space, the purchase and maintenance of storage equipment and fulfillment systems adds to the overhead costs of maintaining inventory. Such equipment may include conveyor belts, fork lift trucks, containers, boxes, cartons and the other hardware that may be necessary to store, pack and ship inventory.

INSURANCE, UTILITIES AND TAXES

Whether storage space allocated to inventory maintenance is rented or owned by a business, certain cost factors should be included in overhead such as insurance, utilities and taxes. The cost of insurance would include fire, theft and water damage in addition to liability coverage in the event anyone was injured in the building area. Taxes may or may not be a direct expense if the storage is rented; however, the cost of taxes would, in effect, be included in the rental amount.

INVENTORY OBSOLESCENCE, SHRINKAGE AND DAMAGE

At any level in the channel of distribution, from the warehouse of the manufacturer to the display showcase of a retailer, there are risks associated with the possession of inventory in that pilferage can result in a direct reduction of profits. Much of inventory shrinkage is related to employees but may also involve theft of merchandise by outsiders, which may or may not be covered by insurance. Merchandise may also become damaged or shopworn—the cost of which is usually not insured. The resulting spoilage of inventory can result in distress merchandise that is marked down or discarded.

WAREHOUSE AND INVENTORY PERSONNEL

Employees who maintain inventory storage facilities, including receiving and shipping merchandise, are direct costs related to inventory. Unless temporary or part-time employees are hired, the units of manpower are relatively fixed. A small inventory storage facility may have only one employee who is overburdened with work. But the hiring of another full-time employee could double labor costs and underutilize employees if there is not enough work for both.

REDUCING INVENTORY MAINTENANCE COSTS
OF MIDDLEMEN

Any business that stocks inventory will incur most of the costs of inventory maintenance just discussed. As long as products are sold over-the-counter or for immediate delivery to customers, inventory will continually flow through the channel of distribution into widely disbursed storage facilities of distributors, wholesalers and retailers. Any middleman who can sell products for future delivery may be able to use the drop shipping services offered by manufacturers or stocking distributors, for at least part of the products sold. There are middlemen, mail order direct marketers in particular, that have every product drop shipped by a stocking entity. Other middlemen may stock a relatively large part of inventory requirements and have only 10 to 25 percent of the products sold drop shipped by suppliers, which may reduce but not eliminate the direct costs of maintaining a portion of inventory.

Reduction of inventory maintenance costs can have a relationship to the full utilization of existing facilities. As an example, if a mail order company stocks all products sold and current inventory storage capacity is used to the maximum, the only possible means for expanding the product line or total sales would require the addition of storage or warehouse space. It may be possible that the only available space would double current capacity yet would only be 30 percent utilized. Rather than incurring the fixed and variable costs of more warehouse space, the mail order firm could establish the policy that any additional product lines would be supplied by manufacturers or distributors that would drop ship. As a first step, the mail order firm could contact all existing sources of supply to determine if drop shipping services can be offered by the supply source for products currently being stocked, which would result in making more space available in the existing storage facilities.

If a middleman is currently using storage or warehouse facilities to capacity, the use of supply sources that will drop ship products would eliminate the necessity of renting or purchasing additional inventory storage facilities. Some manufacturers and stocking distributors will not drop ship products under any circumstances, and if the mail order firm, as an example, sells such products, there is no escaping the fact that inventory of these products must be stocked. Middlemen, selling for future delivery, should consider using the drop shipping services of every supply source that is willing to do so and, out of necessity, stock inventory of all other products. The percentage of products sold by middlemen but drop shipped by supply sources may vary from as little as 2 percent to 50 percent or more. The number of firms that are willing to provide drop shipping services may be limited by the fact that many manufacturers and stocking distributors will not offer drop shipping services.

On the other hand, a middleman may not use the drop shipping services that are offered by a supply source because it may be more cost effective to stock the product in inventory as opposed to using the drop shipping services of the manufacturer or distributor. Middlemen should evaluate individual products and make a determination as to whether it would be more cost effective to stock inventory, considering all the overhead factors, or to use the drop shipping services offered by supply sources.

SHIFTING COSTS AND MARKETING RISKS OF
INVENTORY THROUGH DROP SHIPPING

Marketing functions along with related costs can be shifted, but they cannot be eliminated. A manufacturer who sells direct to the ultimate retail consumer, in fact functions as both a manufacturer and a retailer. The direct selling manufacturer is assuming the additional role of a retailer—a marketing activity that would normally be performed by separate business entity in the channel of distribution.

A middleman who uses the drop shipping services offered by a manufacturer or stocking distributor, in effect, has shifted the function of stocking inventory and filling orders, which would ordinarily be performed by the middleman, backward through the channel of distribution. The direct costs of inventory maintenance and the filling of orders have been eliminated by the middleman who is utilizing the drop shipping services offered by the supply source. The total cost of inventory maintenance and the filling of orders may not have been eliminated completely, however, because the drop shipper may be compensated for performing drop shipping services by charging middlemen higher prices than usual on products that are drop shipped.

EXTRA COMPENSATION FOR PROVIDING DROP SHIPPING SERVICES

To varying degrees, a manufacturer or distributor who provides drop shipping services may have to incur the costs of extra work space and personnel to fill drop ship orders. As mentioned, the in-the-mail drop shipped price for a product that is offered by a manufacturer may be $24 per single unit and $20 per unit if the middleman stocked the merchandise. In this example, the extra cost of $4 charged to the middleman compensates the manufacturer for providing drop shipping services. If the manufacturer processed 1,000 drop shipped orders for a middleman, the extra $4,000 that is being paid by the middleman for drop shipping services may appear to be a substantial amount. However, the middleman might have to pay much more if an inventory of the product was stocked, packed and shipped from the facilities of the middleman, in addition to incurring all of the many direct costs of inventory maintenance and order fulfillment mentioned before.

Drop shipping does not completely eliminate marketing functions but merely shifts them in a cost effective manner. Manufacturers and middlemen alike should make comparative cost determinations on a product-by-product basis as to the relative benefits of the use of drop shipping as a marketing policy.

DROP SHIPPING TRANSACTION COSTS

The financial aspects related to drop shipping involve both the middleman who initiates drop ship orders and supply sources that provide drop shipping services. Drop shipping can be viewed financially by looking at costs related to the physical possession of inventory and the costs involved in the process of initiating and filling drop shipped orders. The transaction costs related to drop shipping have the same implications as to those incurred in the handling of small or single-unit orders—both of which require the preparation of shipping labels, accounting records and paperwork necessary to complete the order filling process.

DROP SHIPPING TRANSACTION COSTS OF MIDDLEMEN

Usually all individual consumer products are purchased in single units or small quantities by retail consumers, whether the product is sold over-the-counter or by mail order. It would be difficult to compare the transaction costs of a retail clerk in a department store to the same costs of a clerk typing shipping labels or making a computer entry to produce an order and shipping label to be sent to a drop shipper. Considering labor costs, a retail sales clerk may only be able to wait on a relatively small number of customers every hour compared with the number of transactions that could be handled by a typist preparing orders and shipping labels. Mail order firms, whether they stock inventory of all products sold or use the drop shipping services of a manufacturer, are still faced with the identical costs of recording sales transactions and preparing shipping labels.

An order that has been converted by a middleman to a shipping label and transaction record can be processed in two ways. The labels and paperwork can be sent to the supply source that will drop ship the order to the customer of the middleman or sent to the warehouse of the middleman and filled from inventory. If a middleman stocks inventory, there is this question: Is the cost of the stock clerk who picks the merchandise, packages the product and ships the merchandise part of the transaction process of filling orders or part of the cost of inventory maintenance? In an effort to segment costs, the wages of order fulfillment personnel in the warehouse of the middleman should be considered a cost of holding inventory.

TRANSACTION COSTS OF DROP SHIPPERS

When a drop shipper receives orders from middlemen, there are transaction costs involved. The order must be verified, entered in the sales records of the stocking entity, and the shipping label and instructions sent to the warehouse or stockroom of the manufacturer or distributor who is providing drop shipping services. The drop shipper is performing a function that would normally be carried out by a middleman who would stock inventory of the product. Because shipping labels are usually prepared by the middleman upon initiating the drop ship order, the stocking entity still must make a record of the transaction. If the drop shipped products are sold on open account, a monthly bill for all drop shipped orders would be prepared and sent to the middleman. Once the accounting transaction is completed by the drop shipper, the shipping labels and order would be sent to the warehouse or stockroom to be processed by the order fulfillment department. They would pack and drop ship the product using the preaddressed shipping label supplied by the middleman. As mentioned, the drop shipper may pass on some of the order fulfillment and transaction costs to the middleman.

POSTAGE AND TRANSPORTATION COSTS ON DROP SHIPMENTS

Any middleman who stocks inventory and sells for future delivery has to prepay shipping costs on products sold, unless the merchandise is sold on a COD basis. Using the example mentioned before, a product that is stocked by a middleman at a $20 per unit cost may have to pay $1.50 per unit for single-piece third-class mail for a package that may weigh 15 ounces. If the product is drop shipped by a manufacturer or stocking distributor, this $1.50 shipping cost may be built into an in-the-mail drop shipped cost of $24 per unit, or the shipping cost could be added on the drop shipped price to the middleman. The shipping costs charged by the drop shipper are usually the same as the costs that would have been incurred by middlemen who ship from their own inventory.

ALL PRODUCTS DROP SHIPPED FOR MIDDLEMEN

The costs and marketing risks of inventory can be more clearly focused in reference to middlemen who have a manufacturer or stocking distributor drop ship all products sold. Such a middleman fits the definition of a true limited-function middleman but is limited only to the extent that they do not stock inventory. There are no direct inventory maintenance costs for a warehouse, storage, or fulfillment system by middlemen who utilize the drop shipping services of suppliers. The middleman may have to pay higher prices for single-unit drop shipments, as compared to the prices for the same products that might be stocked as inventory, but the fixed costs of warehouse and storage space, along with the personnel necessary to operate a fulfillment system are eliminated. In addition, the middleman does not have to pay for products that are drop shipped until after they are sold.

It has been said that middlemen should not be "emotionally involved" with the products sold. It is considered desirable if a retailer of sporting goods or hardware is interested in these product lines, but a person who opens a retail store solely on an emotional involvement with the products may be destined to failure. To expand on this concept, middlemen can avoid physical involvement with inventory through the function of drop shipping and concentrate on the sales, advertising and marketing of products, rather than incurring the expense of purchasing, storing and shipping merchandise. Why large mail order firms point with pride to their 200,000- to 400,000-square-foot warehouses is subject to question, particularly when their customers never see these facilities and have little concern as to whether the products they order are shipped from an inventory held by the seller or drop shipped by the manufacturer. The capital a direct marketer may tie up in inventory, warehouse space and order fulfillment systems may find better and more productive use in the promoting and selling of products through direct response advertising in catalogs, publications or direct mail.

INVENTORY MISMANAGEMENT AND BANKRUPTCY

A mail order firm can get into financial difficulty in two quick ways: if an advertising campaign fails to generate enough orders, or the revenues are not large enough to pay for the advertising, let alone inventory. In this case, the direct marketer may owe the advertising agency or printer a great deal of money. The inventory required to fill orders, based on advertising, may be far less than the quantity ordered from vendors, resulting in overstocks and unsold merchandise that can virtually drive a middleman into bankruptcy, based on demands for payment from supply sources.

Numerous major mail order firms have gone out of business. All of them owed substantial sums to manufacturers and distributors of the products sold. In the late 1950s, a major direct marketer located in northern New Jersey started with virtually no capitalization and over several years was producing a rotogravure catalog with print production runs in the millions. Most of the manufacturers in the United States who produced items that could be sold by mail were anxious to sell products to this successful direct marketer. The marketer eventually went bankrupt without paying for large quantities of merchandise. During the late 1960s, another mail order firm based in New York City started out with little capital and specialized in placing mail order advertising in major newspapers. The firm finally went bankrupt, leaving a long list of creditors.

Another major mail order firm in Boston had been in business for over a hundred years and produced catalogs with press runs in the tens of millions. Many manufacturers were constantly attempting to have their products included in the mail order catalog of this firm, often with little success, since most of the products sold were imported, unbranded novelties, toys or gift items. All of a sudden, the mail order firm started issuing purchase orders to hundreds of manufacturers and distributors in the United States. The purchase orders were impressive—with references and D-U-N-S numbers indicated on all correspondence. Many manufacturers responded to the purchase orders by shipping large quantities of products to the mail order firm. Although there was no direct evidence, it appeared that the firm was already bankrupt, yet the firm continued to order from vendors with no intent to advertise or pay for the merchandise. The mail order firm was evidently acquiring inventory to convert the merchandise into cash as distress merchandise to pay off other creditors that were more important than the vendors who supplied the inventory. None of the manufacturers or distributors that were owed money by this mail order firm received any payment as a result of the bankruptcy proceedings.

In another case, a mail order firm went bankrupt, and 20,000 customers were owed over $800,000 in refunds in addition to $3 million owed to vendors of merchandise. When appointees of the bankruptcy court attempted to take inventory out of the warehouse of the mail order firm, it was empty. Top management of the company had removed all of the merchandise.

These examples have relevance to the marketing function of drop shipping from the standpoint of the middleman and supply sources. A manufacturer who provides drop shipping services can avoid being involved in the financial difficulties of middlemen in that cash-with-order terms can initially be requested on drop shipped orders. The drop shipper can then offer varying amounts of credit and bill middlemen for drop shipped orders when the mail order firm has established a sound history of prompt payment. The drop shipper also has direct knowledge as to the volume of drop shipped sales made by middlemen and can judge whether it would be advisable to ship inventory to the middleman on open account. Manufacturers and stocking distributors should be leery of inordinately large orders for inventory from any middleman who cannot produce a record of sales and financial stability.

On the other hand, if a mail order firm or middleman promotes products that are drop shipped by the supply source, and the advertising or catalog promotions do not produce enough sales, the only entity that will incur the loss is the direct marketer or perhaps advertising media or a printer. If a direct marketer offers to sell products via mail order under a drop ship arrangement and fails to forward orders to the supply source, the postal authorities will soon be aware of this condition through consumer complaints. While drop shipping is not a panacea for the marketing of all products for future delivery, the function of drop shipping as a marketing policy has solid validity, particularly in the area of inventory management, since the inventory required exactly matches the number of orders received.

11

Drop Shipping and Direct Response Advertising

DIRECT MAIL AND MAIL ORDER

Dozens of relatively new books offer valuable guidelines for the content and production of mail order advertising, direct mail and catalogs. The topics covered include marketing strategy, advertising copy, illustrations, product photography graphic presentation, catalog and direct mail formats, media selection and many other aspects of direct response marketing. These books should be used as further references on these subjects as it is not the purpose of this book to cover all aspects of direct response product promotion. However, a large percentage of the most popular books on mail order and direct marketing do not even mention the subject of drop shipping, while others refer to it in only two or three sentences. Even the most authoritative books on inventory management and product fulfillment systems virtually ignore the subject of drop shipping as an alternative to building bigger, better and more efficient warehouses and inventory handling and storage systems, perhaps because of the mind set of many direct marketers that all products sold must be stocked in inventory.

All things being equal, it would be desirable to be able to finance all of the costs of stocking inventory of every product sold and to ship goods immediately from the inventory held by the direct marketer. However, in the complex marketplace of today, all things are not equal, and drop shipping may provide the competitive edge for marketers who want to concentrate on selling and promoting products rather than being preoccupied with the problems of inventory maintenance and fulfillment. Middlemen should look outward and concentrate on the vast market for products, rather than inward to the problems of sagging inventory storage shelves or the breakdown of a forklift truck. Retailers who sell over-the-counter can never escape the constant problems with inventory storage, reorder points, warehouses, store display cases, point-of-purchase material, store interiors, retail clerk personnel difficulties and the many other aspects of selling products at retail in stores.

As mentioned elsewhere, one of the great unknowns in direct response marketing is determining the actual number of total orders for a product that may result from any one advertisement or catalog. A 5-inch advertisement may appear in a consumer publication with a circulation of 2 million, offering a product by mail that retails for $20. How much inventory should the direct marketer stock in inventory in anticipation of the orders that can be expected? Should the mail order company order a gross, 2 gross or 1,000 units of the product? Assuming that the advertisement creates only enough sales to represent 25 percent of the inventory purchased to fill orders, how will the remaining inventory be sold? If the advertisement is marginally successful to the extent that gross sales just pay for the cost of the advertisement, the direct marketer is faced with the problem of disposing of the balance of the inventory. Another advertisement could be placed in the same or another publication with the hope that the balance of the inventory will be sold. If it appears that the product cannot be profitably sold via direct response advertising, the direct marketer may in fact be left with an inventory of products that may take many months to convert into sales. The manufacturer may or may not have a returned merchandise policy, and if that is the case, the price offered to the mail order company will no doubt be lower than the price originally paid for the merchandise. Mail order advertisements and catalogs usually produce sales results that are continually out of balance with the inventory on hand.

DROP SHIPPERS PROVIDE VALUABLE SERVICES

Product sources that drop ship provide a valuable service to direct marketers, even if the middleman stocks inventory of the merchandise. If the number of orders is slightly more than the inventory on hand, the last few orders can be drop shipped by the product source, eliminating the need for purchasing additional inventory. The other obvious benefit of having merchandise sources that drop ship concerns the fact that orders may far exceed available inventory on a timely basis. Orders for a product may flow in at a rate that cannot be filled from current inventory. The delay in having additional inventory shipped from the manufacturer to the direct marketer may be great. By the time additional supplies of merchandise are received and reshipped to the customers of the direct marketer, the

30 Day Mail Order Rule may have long expired, which could cause customer complaints and the resulting costs of notifying consumers of the delay in shipment. Stocking entities that drop ship may provide faster delivery of products to customers than if the merchandise was shipped from the inventory held by the direct marketer. The manufacturer or drop shipper no doubt has the largest centralized inventory of the product in existence, and the chances of nonfulfillment by a drop shipper are unlikely, based on inventory shortages. If an East Coast mail order firm has a drop shipping source in California, and an order is received from a customer in Oregon, the order could be sent via first-class mail to the product source in California and drop shipped to the customer of the middleman in Oregon. The customer would no doubt receive the product faster than if it were sent by parcel post from the East Coast.

Mail order and direct response advertising usually starts with the selection of a product or group of products that a direct response marketer believes can be sold profitably. When possible, it would serve the best interests of a mail order firm to select products of a manufacturer or stocking middleman who offers drop shipping services, even though the mail order company may stock inventory of the merchandise. Accordingly, the drop shipping services offered by a product source should be one of the criteria in selecting products for mail order or direct response promotion.

PRODUCT SELECTION AND PROMOTION

The variety and number of products that are available for promotion is extensive. The number of items among that group that are offered on a drop ship basis is also so great that it may become difficult to determine what direction to pursue in the selection of products to advertise. The product sources listed in past issues of *Drop Shipping News*, as an example, offer drop ship information on many diverse classifications of consumer goods. Direct marketers usually promote a group of similar products in an effort to segment merchandise usage or features to match a segmented market. Some product groups such as general gifts and household gadgets are perhaps product candidates for the catalog promotions of large mail order firms that produce millions of direct mail pieces per year and use a shotgun approach to product marketing. The products listed in a general mail order catalog have such broad appeal that perhaps everyone in the country could have potential use for at least a few of the products listed. Many often contain unbranded products that have mass appeal. The mail order companies that produce these catalogs with multimillion press runs are large enough to send their catalogs to the general public. These huge mail order firms may send unsolicited catalogs to every household in a specific geographic area, based on the average incomes of the residents or "wealthy" zip codes.

In addition, the large mail order firms may rent mailing lists of hundreds of thousands of mail order buyers to be recipients of the mail order catalog. In other cases, large mail order firms may swap unduplicated mailing lists with other mail order firms. Since many of the products listed in such catalogs may be unbranded, low-cost imports, it is not possible to determine what percentage of these products may be drop shipped by the product source. But in most cases the products are usually stocked as inventory by the mail order firms that incur the tremendous overhead of maintaining merchandise warehouses and order fulfillment systems. Many direct marketers do not fall into the category of the large mail order house and are better able to use product and market segmentation as a means of producing profitable sales results.

PRODUCT AND ADVERTISING MEDIA SEGMENTATION

From the standpoint of the demographics of print media readership, product choices for promotion can be developed by working backward from media data. A consumer-oriented magazine on photography exists because there are enough subscribers interested in the subject of photography, and the media can offer a great deal of statistics and readership information to aid potential advertisers. With the editorial content of a consumer photography magazine well defined, the question arises as to what types of products would appeal to the readership of such a publication. Photographic products such as cameras, film processing, enlargers and projectors are the obvious candidates for mail order product promotion in this type of publication, however there are other product groups, slightly off the beaten track of photography, that might also appeal to the readership of this type of magazine.

The other approach uses the product as the starting point. All the features and consumer benefits of the merchandise can define the demographics and interest profile of the ultimate consumer. Media in the form of magazines, direct mail or newspapers can be selected to match product features to the largest group of potential customers, based on inter-media cost comparisons. If a product has features that would appeal to the photographic market, comparisons can be made between the media costs of a number of consumer photographic magazines and the cost of sending expanded advertising literature through a direct mail campaign to a list of known photography enthusiasts. In the first case we state: Here is an excellent print advertising media in the form of a magazine. What products can be profitably advertised and sold to this audience or readership? In the second instance: Here is a product with these features and consumer benefits. Where can the product be advertised and sold profitably through direct response advertising?

DIRECT RESPONSE MEDIA SELECTION

As far as media selection is concerned, direct marketers should have access to the Standard Rate and Data directories covering consumer magazines, business publications and mailing lists, even though advertising may be placed through an advertising agency. Any print media suggestions made by an advertising agency should be reviewed prior to committing advertising dollars. Standard Rate and Data publications are available from Standard Rate and Data Service, Inc., 3004 Glenview Road, Wilmette, IL 60691. Because advertising rates may change rapidly, it may be advisable to subscribe to these directories, if they are not available in a local library. Since the names and addresses of publications change relatively slowly, even an outdated SRDS directory will usually indicate accurate information as to how to contact various publications to gain current advertising rate cards, media kits and production requirements, which are available without charge from the magazine publishers.

The SRDS directory of business publications contains data on major trade magazines that cover virtually every known consumer product group. As mentioned, most of the trade magazines may publish a directory of manufacturers, distributors and importers represented by the segmented classification of consumer products covered by the trade magazine. These same manufacturers that are listed in trade directories may spend millions of dollars on indirect or general advertising in consumer magazines that are listed in a separate SRDS directory. The manufacturers hope that such general advertising in consumer publications will "pull" their products through the channel of distribution that is composed of subscribers to the publications listed in the SRDS directory of business publications. There is the obvious possibility that a direct marketer of any size, including new mail order firms in particular, could match the product sources available in the directories of segmented products published by trade magazines with their counterpart in the form of consumer magazines that closely match the segmented product group of the manufacturers. As an example, a photographic product manufacturer may have been contacted through a listing in a trade magazine directory, and a mail order firm may place direct response advertising in the very same consumer publication used by the manufacturer for their own general or indirect response advertising.

STOCKLESS DIRECT MARKETING

There are successful direct marketers who never stock inventories of products. All products they sell are drop shipped by manufacturers or stocking distributors. A few exceptions may concern products that are so profitable that they are promoted through advertising or catalog listings, even though the supply source will not drop ship the item. Firms that promote any or all products that are available on a drop ship basis use drop shipping as the criteria for product selection. As a result, the products that are drop shipped may be so diverse in nature that it may be difficult to segment products into groups to match a segmented market. As a result, a catalog produced by a mail order firm that promotes drop shipped products may include housewares, sporting goods, gifts, consumer electronics and a wide cross-section of items. In spite of the diversity of products listed in such a catalog, there is a good possibility that it could be successful.

In a further refinement, there is the possibility of combining product segmentation along with the use of product sources that provide drop shipping services. A direct marketer may decide to produce a catalog of sporting goods—all of which are to be supplied by sources that drop ship individual orders. A mailing list of all of the sporting goods manufacturers and major importers could be used as the basis for a letter of inquiry to these product sources, specifically requesting drop shipping information. Of the hundreds of sporting goods manufacturers, there would no doubt be enough manufacturers who would offer drop shipping services. On that basis a catalog of sporting goods could be designed, with each and every item drop shipped by the manufacturer or stocking distributor. By eliminating all the costs and risks of inventory, the direct marketer can direct the use of assets and efforts into promoting and selling products and utilize the drop shipping services of the supply source for product order fulfillment.

BUILDING CUSTOMER LISTS VIA
DROP SHIPPED PRODUCTS

Most direct marketers sell an assortment of products that are related, based on the segmented or specialized interests of potential customers. A catalog of fishing gear may include rods, reels, lures, line, hooks, tackle boxes and the hundreds of other items that might appeal to the fisherman. Product segmentation can then allow a direct marketer to closely select an advertising medium such as magazines, radio, television or newspapers or to use direct mail advertising through the rental or compilation of a mailing list. The direct marketer who has prepared a catalog of fishing gear can mail the literature to a mailing list of known fishermen.

Mail order firms can often build their own mailing list data base of potential customers via space advertisements in publications. If the mail order firm produces a sixteen- or thirty-two-page catalog of items that would appeal to the fisherman, a small space advertisement in a related publication could offer the catalog free of charge to readers. The mail order firm could also design a mail order advertisement for a name-brand fishing reel at a very competitive price and have the reels drop shipped by the manufacturer or stocking distributor, along with the offer to send a free catalog of other fishing gear products. The sales of reels that result from the small space advertisement might create a profit or at least build a mailing list base for other direct mail offers. Since the actual number of orders that will be generated by any mail order advertisement is unknown, having orders drop shipped by the supply source insures that orders can be filled promptly with the exact quantity of inventory required.

DROP SHIPPING OFFERS FLEXIBILITY IN TESTING MAIL ORDER PRODUCTS

Direct marketers or mail order firms that place advertisements in print media magazines run the risk of not being able to determine sales volume with any great accuracy. A specialized mail order product section of a Sunday newspaper supplement may have a circulation of over a million readers, but the direct marketer still must decide on the quantity of an initial inventory to stock in anticipation of orders. Whether the direct marketer places advertising directly with publications or through an advertising agency, the closing date for insertion orders may be as long as two to perhaps three months in advance for some magazines. Some weeks before the publication is distributed, an inventory of products must be purchased and made ready to fill orders. The supply source may require the purchase of a standard pack of the product that may be 72 or 144 units as a minimum order. The mail order firm is therefore committed to purchasing these quantities, regardless of the number of orders received. The direct marketer not only has to pay for the inventory immediately but may end up with a large supply of unsold merchandise.

Until a pattern of order response can be established through the test marketing of a mail order product, perhaps drop shipping can offer the flexibility in inventory requirements that allows the number of orders received to exactly match the inventory needed to fill orders—right down to the very last unit with no shortages or excess stock. If the sales results indicate that the product can be profitably sold via direct response advertising, then it may be advantageous to stock the product in inventory, but by doing so the mail order firm incurs all of the marketing costs and risks of physical possession of inventory, as mentioned previously.

As a marketing policy, the mail order firm may use a combination of stocking and using drop shipping services of the supply source. If there are significant cost advantages in stocking the minimum quantity of inventory required by the manufacturer or distributor, then it may be beneficial to stock seventy-two units, a gross or several gross of the product in anticipation of orders. The initial orders received from the mail order promotion could then be filled from inventory held by the mail order company, and it may be possible to judge the level of response to the advertising to make a decision to order and stock additional inventory or to have the balance of orders drop shipped by the supply source. It is important that the manufacturer or stocking distributor will in fact agree to drop ship single units at a stated price, even though the mail order firm, selling for future delivery, stocks the product in inventory.

RENTING MAILING LISTS OF POTENTIAL CUSTOMERS

The most authoritative source for information on mailing lists is the Standard Rate and Data Service *Direct Mail List Rates and Data*, 3004 Glenview Road, Wilmette, IL 60691. This directory lists source information on every conceivable type of consumer mailing list that is usually offered for one-time rental at prices that range from $20 per thousand to $100 per thousand for very exclusive names and addresses. Lists are supplied on computer printouts, gummed stock or pressure-sensitive labels. Rented mailing lists of potential customers can be pinpointed to specific interests of the listees or based on previous purchases from a particular type of mail order catalog. Available mailing lists also include subscribers to various types of consumer magazines that may form the basis for a direct mail campaign. Direct marketers may already have a catalog of specific products, and the direct mail advertising managers of most firms can select mailing lists that would offer the greatest sales potential.

This approach to direct mail is used when the company already has an existing catalog, and the task of selecting the most productive mailing list to be recipients of the catalog is usually based on the known interests or past purchases of the listees. Another method of using highly selective mailing lists is to examine the demographics and buying profile of specific lists and then develop a catalog or direct mail campaign promoting a specific group of products that would most closely match the interests of potential buyers on the list.

TELEVISION SHOPPING SERVICES

There has been a large increase in direct response television programming, particularly on cable TV. The number of firms selling a variety of consumer products has increased rapidly. They sell millions of dollars worth of merchandise weekly. By using 800 toll-free numbers, buyers can phone their orders in and charge purchases to any one of several national credit cards. Rather than pay for individual advertisements, the shopping services contract for relatively large segments of television time, often running into many hours of programming. Products are offered, one after another, with the aid of demonstrators or product promotion representatives who urge the public to phone in orders. Large staffs of telephone operators record the incoming orders and process them for fulfillment. Although there are no industry statistics on the subject, most of the products sold through home shopping services are supplied from inventory held by the seller, which involves all costs of purchasing, storing and filling orders, along with the necessary personnel to perform these tasks. There is no doubt that a good portion of the consumer products sold via home shopping service television promotions could be drop shipped by the product source. As in the case of the very large mail order firms, most home shopping services no doubt have extensive amounts of costly inventory stored in large warehouses ready for fulfillment.

CONSUMER PRODUCT BUYING SERVICES

A consumer product buying service is a method of selling products for future delivery through the use of drop shipping, although the psychology of the buyer and seller is slightly different from that of a regular retail store and their customers. The buying service can usually offer low, competitive prices on products because the service does not stock inventory and accordingly has very low overhead. Instead of promoting individual or groups of related products, the buying service will often sell any type of product that can be identified by a manufacturer's model or stock number and has a price high enough to justify the time and effort to handle the order. The buying public usually knows that the buying services do not have inventory of the product and that the product will be shipped by the manufacturer or distributor.

As an example, a buying service located in New York City works through a number of social and membership organizations. As a service to their members, these organizations promote the buying service in bulletins or newsletters. The members can come into the offices of the buying service to look at catalog sheets or go to a local retailer to determine the model and stock number of the desired products. In effect, regular retail stores act as the showroom for the buying service. The consumer then contacts the buying service for a quotation on the model and stock number of the product. Since many manufacturers identify products by stock number in factory-sealed cartons, the buying service may publish a list of products by model number and price. The concept of a buying service could be added to an existing retail store or as a division of a mail order company.

In most instances, the buying service does not have the expense of printing product literature or catalogs because the consumers have already determined what make and model of the product they want to purchase. A buying service is very compatible with drop shipping in that it is understood by the consumer that the seller does not have an inventory of the product in stock, and the service is performed by buying the product on special order. The consumer is aware that the buying service will forward the order to a source of supply that will in turn drop ship the product to the customer. The buying service may restrict the types of products sold to major appliances and consumer electronics and have made arrangements with the manufacturers or large regional distributors to provide drop shipping services.

MAIL ORDER CATALOG AND ADVERTISING PROMOTIONS

The sale of products for future delivery can be accomplished by mail order advertising, catalogs, direct mail, radio, television, buying services, telemarketing, special orders in stores and a number of other direct marketing techniques. Numerous books on all of these subjects cover almost every facet of direct response marketing, from marketing plans and strategies, advertising copy, graphics, design of advertisements, production of catalogs and direct mail formats to the dozens of other aspects of product promotion through print media and electronic communication. Most of these books are very valuable, and each may have a slightly different approach to the same goal: the production of direct response advertising that will produce profitable results. However, the theory and practice of producing profitable direct response marketing programs in the form of advertising does not as such have a direct bearing on the use of drop shipping as a marketing function. A catalog of products or a mail order advertisement in a publication states the availability of the products offered, without reference as to whether the order fulfillment will be made from inventory held by the seller or if it will be drop shipped by the manufacturer or a stocking distributor. Since the purpose of this book is to examine all facets of drop shipping as a marketing function, it would be better left to other books to offer expanded concepts on advertising copy, graphics and the production of mail order and direct response advertising.

12

Economic Aspects of
Drop Shipping

ROLE OF DROP SHIPPING OBSCURED BY LACK OF DATA

It would be difficult to determine whether drop shipping as a marketing function has had any major impact on order fulfillment and product distribution. If the outdated definition of a drop shipper is used as the basis for marketing or economic analysis, it is true that the sales volume of a small group of desk jobbers or limited-function middlemen would be an infinitesimal part of the gross national product. As mentioned in chapter 1, the organizations that attempt to record the volume of business done by various types of businesses often lack data on quality and quantity. This is particularly true if the figures represent drop shippers as a group of limited-function middlemen or parlor jobbers who take title to goods but not physical possession and specialize in the distribution of coal, lumber and other bulky products. If this concept of the function of drop shipping is the basis for defining the volume of business transacted as drop shipments, then it is clear that this definition of drop shipping applies only to a very small group of highly specialized limited-function middlemen.

Drop shipping is a marketing function that involves many types of wholesalers, distributors and retailers. The total volume of sales made on a drop ship basis nationally is vastly greater than the sales made by a small group of desk or parlor jobbers dealing in bulky items. In addition, the data on the volume of business transacted as drop shipments are further obscured by the fact that those organizations, including governmental agencies, that collect sales volume statistics of various industries or by types of middlemen often look at total sales. They make no reference as to whether the products sold were shipped from inventory held by the middleman or drop shipped by a supply source such as the manufacturer or stocking distributor. Organizations that collect and interpret sales volume statistics no doubt assume that the sales made by functional middlemen are based on shipments of products held as inventory by these business entities. It would seem logical to come to this conclusion because there is no evidence they used any other method of product fulfillment such as drop shipping.

From a macro economic standpoint it would be very difficult to isolate the sales volume handled as drop shipments on a national basis. Research into the scope and volume of business transacted through the marketing function of drop shipping is also complicated by the fact that there are hundreds of thousands of privately held firms acting as functional middlemen. They are required to provide only a single sales figure on confidential business tax returns, which are never made public.

In addition, firms of all sizes would probably not want to incur the costs involved in making an analysis of the volume of orders handled as drop shipments as opposed to sales shipped from held inventory. If such sales analyses were made by middlemen, the results would seldom flow into public records. Nor would information be available on volume of business transacted as drop shipments—provided there was even a large enough sample to make statistical projections to a specific line of trade or industry. Perhaps the only means for defining the sales volume of business transacted through drop shipping on a national basis would be "small" or a relatively minor part of total sales volume. However, drop shipping does exist in the marketplace, and the scope of drop shipping is far greater than the limiting definition of sales made through a desk jobber. As a matter of fact, the inadequate statistics that are available vastly underestimate the role of drop shipping in the economy, even though the value of drop shipped transactions cannot be accurately defined.

VALUE AND VOLUME OF SALES AS A MEASURE OF DROP SHIPPING ACTIVITY

Orders that are processed through the function of drop shipping could be defined on the dollar value of the products drop shipped or the sheer volume of orders, as a means for measuring the scope of drop shipping in the economy. It is well established that many functional middlemen, particularly those that may distribute heavy industrial equipment or machinery, take title to the products sold, rather than acting as an agent or sales representative for the manufacturer. It is also obvious that 50-ton plastic injection molding machines or huge printing presses are not stored in the inventory of the middlemen prior to delivery to customers. The dollar value of much of this type of equipment could run into the many hundreds of thousands of dollars. There is also the possibility that the manufacturer of such machinery may be located in Europe or other parts of the world, and shipment is being made by ocean freight in cargo containers that would only fit on a tractor trailer truck. Without having access to the sales records of this type of middleman, it is safe to say that the bulk of all such products are drop shipped to the factory or plant of the customer of the middleman.

The cost savings offered by eliminating the necessity of temporarily storing such heavy and expensive equipment by a middleman could represent the entire profit to be made on the sale. There are dozens of other types of products and industries where the dollar value of products that are drop shipped represent high-ticket items. In the equipment example, drop shipping provides a practical solution to order fulfillment, based on the type of middleman, available facilities for storage and the nature of the products involved. The savings offered by the elimination of double handling of the machinery, added transportation costs, rigging, warehouse charges and the cost of personnel could no doubt be determined for each company but the cumulative total value of the savings resulting from all such drop shipping transactions on a yearly basis throughout the country would be difficult to document.

Another factor that could add to the scope of drop shipping in the economy relates to the potentially large volume of drop shipments performed as a result of one transaction. It was not unusual for a firm that grew miniature lemon and orange trees in Florida to drop ship single units of up to 500,000 trees under a contract that included the time necessary to grow the trees. Other examples could include direct marketers and mail order companies that have many thousands of orders drop shipped by supply sources; however, the value of these drop shipments remains hidden in the sales records of literally hundreds of thousands of middlemen.

The use of drop shipping as a marketing function is a matter of degree in that truly limited-function middlemen, including some mail order firms, may deal exclusively in drop shipments and never stock inventory of any products. Accurate data on the scope and sales volume of such limited-function middlemen are not available from any known reliable source. In addition, full-function middlemen may stock varying quantities of inventory from which they ship or transfer the products to their customers, while the balance of other orders are drop shipped by the supply source. The percentage of products that is stocked by full-function middlemen might be as low as 50 percent or as high as 99 percent, with the reciprocal of these percentage figures representing orders that are drop shipped by manufacturers or stocking distributors. The true value of all products drop shipped on a yearly basis in the United States is unknown.

ECONOMIC TIME AND PLACE UTILITIES

From a total economic viewpoint, storage of inventory is the function that gives products "place utility." Once a product takes a three-dimensional "form utility" as finished goods produced by a manufacturer, the value added by place utility flows through the channel of distribution until the product is finally sold to the ultimate consumer or end user. The manufacturer who produces inventory cannot escape the initial marketing costs and risks associated with providing storage facilities for that inventory. The costs and marketing risks of the maintenance and warehousing of inventory have been discussed in previous chapters.

Under ordinary circumstances, as physical possession of products moves toward the ultimate consumer or end user, each successive type of functional middleman provides place utility by storing inventory. The quantities of individual products usually become less concentrated as they become physically closer to the ultimate consumer, but are more disbursed on a geographic basis. The total costs of the physical possession of goods are continually being shifted through the channel of distribution, and the cumulative costs of inventory maintenance are included in the ever-increasing price of the products. Time and place utilities in a sense flow hand-in-hand through the distribution channel.

If at any level in the channel of distribution the requirement to store or warehouse inventory is eliminated, all of the direct costs associated with inventory maintenance are eliminated too with some sacrifice of both place and time utilities. At least on the retail store level, inventory maintenance is required to have products available to sell at the right place and at the right time. If the products are still being held by the manufacturer or stocking distributor, the products are in the wrong place at the wrong time, as far as any possibility to sell the products over-the-counter is concerned. However, if the products can be sold for future delivery, through mail order promotion or other means, then the time and place utilities for products are of much less importance if the fulfillment process can be shifted backward through the channel of distribution and accomplished through the function of drop shipping.

As stated previously, consumers pay a tremendous price for the privilege of having a wide variety of products available for sale over-the-counter. The economic function of time and place utility adds billions of dollars to the cost of all products sold, including both consumer and industrial products. Some product groups cannot be sold for future delivery, as in the case of groceries and other food items. Other consumer goods, such as those sold in department or specialty stores, are usually sold over-the-counter with all of the built-in costs associated with inventory maintenance and retailing. These same products in theory could be sold through a catalog via mail order marketing methods for future delivery. Under these conditions, there would be no need to have an inventory of products on hand if the supply source provides drop shipping services.

MEASUREMENT OF ECONOMIC SAVINGS THROUGH DROP SHIPPING

When considering the total economy, it would be difficult to apply any measure of savings that would result from the function of drop shipping. If every functional middleman had to stock every single unit of product as it flowed through the channel of distribution, there would no doubt be an increase in the total economic need for warehouse and storage space, but there is no means for determining the costs involved. Using a previous example, the distributor of 50-ton plastic injection molding machines would be required to have a warehouse to receive shipment of the machinery, temporarily store the equipment and then reship the product to the industrial user. Considering the economic costs of the warehouse facilities that would be required to accommodate such transactions on a national basis, it becomes evident that a great deal of additional storage or warehouse space would be required in the United States along with all of the associated costs of land and building construction. Other aspects of not using drop shipping have been discussed elsewhere in this book and include among others the double handling of machinery, labor and transportation costs. The direct costs just mentioned would not be incurred through the use of drop shipping.

SHIFTING ECONOMIC COSTS OF INVENTORY

If a manufacturer or stocking distributor provides drop shipping services, business entities are holding inventory that would normally have been shifted physically to full-function middlemen. The role of inventory maintenance can be considered to be retained by the manufacturer or stocking distributor or shifted backward from the functional middleman. If the stocking entity is providing drop shipping services for a large number of middlemen, more warehouse space and facilities may have to be provided than would be necessary if the manufacturer or stocking distributor was only selling to full-function middlemen who took possession of inventory. The inventory storage function that would have been performed by middlemen has not been eliminated through the use of drop shipping but has instead been retained by the manufacturer or distributor who is performing drop shipping services.

The direct costs of inventory maintenance have been eliminated by middlemen who use the drop shipping services provided by a manufacturer. These fixed, direct costs of inventory maintenance may include the owning or renting of warehouse space, insurance, protection and personnel. If a middleman has all products drop shipped, there is no need to have any storage or warehouse space. While the direct costs of inventory maintenance may be eliminated or vastly reduced, as mentioned, there can still be indirect costs of inventory maintenance that are paid for by the middleman through higher unit prices for single-unit drop shipped orders than if the merchandise was stocked as inventory. Drop shippers no doubt pass on the costs of the actual shipping charges to middlemen on drop shipped orders, in addition to other costs incurred by the drop shipper for performing services for middlemen. The real economies of drop shipping from the viewpoint of the middleman occur because the total extra costs paid to the supply source for performing drop shipping services may be substantially less than the total cost of stocking the same inventory of the products sold. As an example, it may cost a middleman $60,000 a year to rent and staff a warehouse, while it might cost only $10,000 a year in extra costs paid to drop shippers to fill single-unit orders. Although inventory maintenance costs have not been completely eliminated, drop shipping may reduce such costs substantially.

Perhaps the only way to analyze the cost effectiveness of drop shipping is company by company and product by product to determine measurable savings. In addition, the transaction costs of processing drop ship orders should be compared to the costs involved in processing orders for fulfillment from the inventory held by the middleman. In the final analysis, the effectiveness and economic benefits of drop shipping are directly related to the costs of stocking products or having them drop shipped by a supply source. Examples of the factors used to measure these cost differentials were outlined in chapter 10 of this book.

THE ROLE OF COST ACCOUNTING

Cost accountants can usually determine with accuracy the unit costs of producing a finished product. Cost accounting methods are perhaps the best way to determine the potential savings from drop shipping services compared to purchasing inventory to be stored by the middleman. Some direct marketers may find little difficulty in determining the cost differential between these costs. It may be more difficult to make a financial comparison between any added charges made by drop shippers for performing this function and all of the fixed and variable costs of maintaining warehouse or storage facilities and stocking inventory of the products sold by middlemen.

ADVANTAGES OF DROP SHIPPING BY MANUFACTURERS

The following list of advantages to stocking entities that provide drop shipping services is partially based on the results of the survey of 400 drop shippers mentioned in chapter 3. The advantages can be projected to any type of firm that stocks merchandise or product inventory.

1. The drop shipper or stocking entity may gain additional business by offering drop shipping services to middlemen.

2. Sales can be made to middlemen who would not ordinarily be able to stock all of the products offered by the manufacturer.

3. Distribution of products may be gained at the expense of competitors.

4. A good portion of the cost of any consumer advertising can be shifted to middlemen who promote the products in catalogs or publications.

5. Additional profits on drop shipped orders may be gained by extending smaller-than-usual discounts on such orders.

6. Savings may be made by reducing the total initial investment in inventory, since middlemen use the same inventory for the fulfillment of all drop shipped orders.

7. Billing and credit extensions may be eliminated, if cash-with-order terms are required on drop shipped orders.

8. Marketing costs may be reduced when introducing new products, by producing a small, centralized inventory that is more closely linked to consumer demand, rather than filling a channel of distribution.

9. If extra charges are imposed for providing drop shipping services for middlemen, the function could become a profit center.

10. Proper packaging and shipment of drop shipped orders may reduce damaged goods and refund requests.

11. The number of drop shipped orders received along with the known advertising efforts of middlemen may provide the basis for marketing research into the areas of market and sales potentials for the product and as an aid in production planning.

12. Syndicated catalogs or product literature could be sold to middlemen for their imprint or reprint. Product advertising copy, photography and graphics supplied by the drop shipper may be of higher quality than could be produced by individual middlemen.

DISADVANTAGES OF PROVIDING DROP SHIPPING SERVICES BY MANUFACTURERS

The bulk of all goods are sold direct to middlemen who take physical possession of goods, indicating that there are disadvantages in providing drop shipping services as follows:

1. The very nature of the product may not be compatible with drop shipping. The product may be perishable, too low in price, difficult to pack and ship, too costly to ship in single units, not adaptable for direct response marketing methods, or mail order promotion or the product may already be widely available in the marketplace.

2. The cost of handling single-unit drop shipments may be too high, even though some or all of these costs could be passed on to middlemen.

3. Providing drop shipping services may require the expansion of warehouse and storage space and the addition of personnel or a special department to provide such services.

4. The transaction costs in the form of record keeping, billing and fulfillment may be higher than the cost advantages of providing drop shipping services.

5. Since drop shipping is an alternate means of product distribution, a policy decision of management not to provide drop shipping may be based on the need to protect middlemen who stock the products of the supply source or for other undefinable, subjective reasons.

ADVANTAGES OF DROP SHIPPING FOR MIDDLEMEN

A functional middleman who can sell products for future delivery may gain a number of advantages by using drop shipping services provided by product sources. The types of products and marketing efforts of middlemen may differ; however, some of the advantages as to the use of drop shipping as a marketing policy of middlemen are as follows:

1. The middleman invests nothing in inventory until after the products are sold.

2. Funds that might have been required to finance inventory can be put to other use, such as advertising and promotion.

3. No direct costs of storage or warehouse facilites are incurred, which would save varying amounts of money, depending on the types of products.

4. No personnel are required to pick, pack and ship merchandise since this function is shifted to the drop shipper.

5. There is no distress merchandise or unsold goods to contend with, since drop shipped orders exactly equal sales. There is no constant imbalance between orders received and inventory on hand, which is the usual condition if merchandise is kept in inventory.

6. Since middlemen who stock inventory usually pay for shipping charges, f.o.b. the source of supply, the value of these shipping charges can be used to offset any extra charges made by the drop shipper for providing services.

7. Extra costs of inventory maintenance such as boxes, shipping supplies, storage racks and conveyer belts are eliminated.

8. The costs of protecting merchandise from pilferage or damage from water, fire or accidents have been eliminated.

9. Any additional charges made by the drop shipper for handling single-unit orders may be offset from savings generated by eliminating the entire storage and fulfillment function.

10. Overall transportation costs may be reduced if the drop shipper is closer to the customer of the middleman.

11. Drop shipped orders may in fact be received sooner by the customers of the middleman, in the event that any inventory held by the middleman was depleted.

12. The economic costs of double handling and transportation have been eliminated with direct financial savings and faster delivery to the customers of the middleman.

13. Management efforts and talents can be concentrated on the sale and promotion of products, rather than on being preoccupied with the problems surrounding the maintenance of inventory.

Depending on the types of products, channel of distribution and other factors, there may be additional benefits gained by middlemen through the use of drop shipping services provided by supply sources.

DISADVANTAGES OF DROP SHIPPING FOR MIDDLEMEN

Many middlemen are forced to stock inventory of every product sold, based on the nature of the channel of distribution or the types of products involved. To a great extent, inventory must be maintained by middlemen because their customers require immediate or over-the-counter delivery of products. Middlemen may also prefer to supply customers from their own inventory, even though drop shipping services may be offered by the supply source. Under these circumstances, drop shipping may be considered a disadvantage to middlemen for the following reasons:

1. The middleman may have a large number of personnel or existing warehouse or storage space that would be underutilized if the firm did not stock inventory

2. The quantity discounts or carload lot pricing offered by the supply source may be so great that it would be cost effective to stock inventory of all products, rather than having the same items drop shipped

3. There may be delays in filling drop shipped orders

4. The customers of the middleman may have less confidence in middlemen who are known not to stock inventory

5. The customers of the middleman may not want to deal with a firm that does not stock inventory because orders would in fact be drop shipped from the supply source

6. The middleman may be well financed and have no difficulty in purchasing and storing inventory

AN ECONOMY WITHOUT DROP SHIPPING

It would require a massive amount of marketing research to determine the dollar value, scope and total impact of drop shipping on the economy. However, some insight into the economic aspects of drop shipping may be offered through subtractive analysis, under the following concept: What if the marketing function of drop shipping did not exist in the marketplace? If all manufacturers and distributors required that their customers (jobbers, wholesalers, dealers and retailers) stock inventory of all the products sold, then the entire function of drop shipping would be eliminated. From the standpoint of the manufacturer, there might be savings in that the personnel and storage space necessary to provide drop shipping services would be eliminated.

In addition, order handling along with accounting and billing might be simplified. There may also be economies regarding standard packaging of minimum quantities and more efficient shipping systems. However, by eliminating drop shipping as a marketing function, the stocking entity may also be eliminating the possibility of selling to or through functional middlemen who would not ordinarily be interested in promoting the products of the supply source, unless drop shipping services were offered.

The advantages and disadvantages of drop shipping from the standpoint of the stocking entity and middleman alike, as mentioned above, indicate areas that could be affected by eliminating drop shipping entirely. Consider the following factors:

Double Handling of Products

If drop shipping were completely eliminated from the economy, then every middleman would have to stock inventories of all products sold. The need for added personnel to handle receiving and reshipping may have an economic impact on the total cost of distributing goods. In chapter 1, an example was given that described the direct factory shipment of an entire trailer truck loaded with air conditioners to a co-op apartment house. The air conditioner dealer never had physical possession of the merchandise. If the order had not been drop shipped to the customer of the dealer, then the truckload of air conditioners would have had to be off-loaded by the personnel of the air conditioner dealer, placed in storage and then reloaded onto delivery trucks owned or rented by the dealer with their own personnel and finally off-loaded at the address of the customer. The double handling of the products in this example involves labor costs, in addition to the costs of a separate delivery truck. This example could be multiplied thousands of times in the marketplace and include numerous types of product classifications such as machinery, raw materials, building materials, food products, in addition to single units of consumer products. The total cost and economic impact of the double handling of orders created by the elimination of drop shipping would be difficult to document, but no doubt significant.

Temporary Use of Storage Facilities

The physical plant and equipment of storage facilities are more or less permanent, but the products contained therein are usually transient because products are continually being shifted from one business entity to another until final delivery is made to the ultimate consumer or end user. If drop shipping were eliminated, all middlemen would have to take physical possession of inventory at every successive level in the channel of distribution. There would no doubt be a demand for more warehouse or storage facilities by wholesalers, jobbers and retailers of all types at very substantial costs. The impact of the cost of such storage space might be related to the fact that usage of such facilities may be temporary or transient.

In the example of the sale of an imported 50-ton plastic injection molding machine by a distributor to a custom injection molding company, the machine would no doubt be off-loaded at the dock from a freighter onto a tractor trailer for delivery direct to the customer of the distributor. If drop shipping did not exist, the distributor would have to take physical possession of the machinery. However, the number of sales of very expensive molding equipment might occur once a month or perhaps every other month. If the distributor was forced to provide temporary storage space for the machinery, the cost of such facilities, whether owned or rented, would have an economic impact on overhead expenses. In addition, the cost of off-loading and then reloading the machinery, perhaps within a day or two, may result in the warehouse space being completely empty 90 percent of the time—an economic waste.

Lower Economic Costs through Drop Shipping

If the use of drop shipping was expanded within the economy, it is possible that there would be less need for additional warehouse or storage space within the channel of distribution. Since every drop shipment bypasses storage facilities of a middleman, it would appear that existing space could be better utilized. In addition, the need for constant unloading and reloading of inventory would be eliminated by the entity that initiates drop shipped orders, along with all the marketing risks associated with the possession of inventory as previously described. Drop shipping as a marketing function may reduce the capital required to build storage or warehouse facilities that may be underutilized or lie empty, only to be used to store presold products that are in effect "in transit" to the customer of the middleman.

LACK OF STATISTICAL DATA

The advantages and disadvantages regarding drop shipping as a marketing function can perhaps be best described in written terms, rather than statistical analysis. The massive amount of marketing research that would be required to determine accurately what percentage of all products sold in the United States are handled as drop shipments—the dollar value of such transactions and the types of products and middlemen involved—would no doubt be of interest but would such statistics serve a practical purpose? If it were possible to determine the economic role of drop shipping in the marketplace, the results might be distilled to hypothetical data indicating that the sale of 18 percent of all machine tools were transacted as drop shipments, 6 percent of consumer products, and 12 percent of industrial products, and so on. Since it appears that there are no accurate data, the assumption might be made that there has not been enough interest in undertaking marketing research projects to determine the impact or usage of drop shipping on a statistical basis, considering the costs that would be involved in producing accurate data. Such studies would perhaps be best left in the hands of trade associations of various industries to poll their membership as to the use of drop shipping within an industry. Governmental agencies or marketing research organizations might also sponsor such research. It is beyond the scope of this book to undertake such economic analysis, other than to offer in descriptive terms some of the advantages, disadvantages and economic implications concerning the use of drop shipping.

CONCLUSION

The number of variables in any marketing program are extensive. It would be difficult to establish that any one marketing policy or method would be adaptable for use by all types of product sources and middlemen. Drop shipping offers advantages and disadvantages for both the drop shipper who provides drop shipping services and middlemen alike. Such factors as the channel of distribution, product types, prices, discounts, delivery time, distance to the customer, transportation and order handling costs and the many other factors outlined within this book may act as a guide for manufacturers, stocking distributors and middlemen of all types as to the use of drop shipping as a marketing policy.

The marketing risks and costs created by the physical possession of inventory have been well documented. As an example, an authority on logistics states:

A shift of stock-keeping responsibility from inventory-conscious retailers to wholesalers and manufacturers has taken place in recent years. This has resulted in part from the desire of retailers to reduce speculation and unsaleable stocks in an age of expanding product lines as well as a realization that warehousing and materials handling costs may be significantly lower per unit for manufacturers and wholesalers than for their retailer customers. In this case, the shift of responsibility for the performance of these functions in the channel of distribution is a logical result of interorganizational analysis and management.[1]

Although the author of this statement fails to mention drop shipping as a possible solution to the problem, the function of drop shipping may in fact reduce the marketing risks of the physical possession of inventory at various levels in the channel of distribution.

NOTE

1. James L. Heskett, "Sweeping Changes in Distribution," *Harvard Business Review* 51 (March–April 1973): 128–129.

Selected Bibliography

Alderson, Wroe. *Dynamic Marketing Behavior*. Homewood, IL: Richard D. Irwin, 1965.

Alexander, Ralph S., James S. Cross, and Richard M. Hill. *Industrial Marketing*. Homewood, IL: Richard D. Irwin, 1963.

Allvine, Fred C. *Marketing Principles and Practices*. San Diego, CA: Harcourt, Brace, Jovanovich, 1987.

Ballinger, Raymond A. *Direct Mail Design*. New York: Reinhold, 1963.

Banning, Douglas. *Techniques for Marketing New Products*. New York: McGraw-Hill Book Company, 1957.

Beckman, Theodore N. "The Value Added Concept as Applied to Marketing and Its Implications." *Frontiers in Marketing Thought*. Bloomington, IN: Bureau of Business Research, Indiana University, 1955.

Beckman, Theodore N., and Nathanael H. Engle. *Wholesaling*. New York: Ronald Press, 1951.

Beckman, Theodore N., and Harold H. Maynard. *Principles of Marketing*, 4th ed. New York: Ronald Press, 1946.

Beckman, Theodore N., Nathanael H. Engle, and Robert D. Buzzell. *Wholesaling*, 3rd ed. New York: Ronald Press Company, 1959.

Beckman, Theodore N., Harold H. Maynard, and William R. Davidson. *Principles of Marketing*, 6th ed. New York: Ronald Press Company, 1957.

Bowersox, Donald J. *Logistical Management*. New York: Macmillan Publishing Company, 1974.

Boyd, Harper W., and Ralph Westfall. *Marketing Research*, 3rd ed., Homewood, IL: Richard D. Irwin, 1972.

Britt, Steuart H., ed. *The Dartnell Marketing Manager's Handbook*. Chicago: Dartnell Corporation, 1973.

Britt, Steuart H., and Harper W. Boyd, Jr. *Marketing Management and Administration in Action*, 3rd ed. New York: McGraw-Hill Book Company, 1973.

Bucklin, Louis P. *Competition and Evolution in the Distributive Trades*. Englewood Cliffs, NJ: Prentice-Hall, 1972.

Buell, Victor P., ed. *Handbook of Modern Marketing*. New York: McGraw-Hill Book Company, 1970.

Buzzell, Robert D., Robert E. Nourse, and John B. Matthews, Jr. *Marketing: A Contemporary Analysis*, 2nd ed. New York: McGraw-Hill Book Company, 1972.

Caples, John. *Tested Advertising Methods*, 4th ed. Englewood Cliffs, NJ: Prentice-Hall, 1974.

Carman, James M., and Kenneth P. Uhl. *Marketing Principles and Methods*, 7th ed. Homewood, IL: Richard D. Irwin, 1973.

Clewett, Richard M., ed. *Marketing Channels for Manufactured Products*. Homewood, IL: Richard D. Irwin, 1954.

Converse, Paul D., Harvey W. Huegy, and Robert V. Mitchell. *Elements of Marketing*, 7th ed. Englewood Cliffs, NJ: Prentice-Hall, 1965.

Cox, Reavis. *Distribution in a High-Level Economy*. Englewood Cliffs, NJ: Prentice-Hall, 1965.

Cox, Reavis, Wroe Alderson, and Stanley J. Shapiro. *Theory in Marketing*. Homewood, IL: Richard D. Irwin, 1964.

Cravens, David W., and Robert B. Woodruff. *Marketing*. Reading, MA: Addison-Wesley, 1986.

Davis, Kenneth R. *Marketing Management*, 3rd ed. New York: Ronald Press Company, 1972.

Dodge, Robert H. *Industrial Marketing*. New York: McGraw-Hill Book Company, 1970.

Evans, Joel R., and Barry Berman. *Marketing*, 3rd ed. New York: John Wiley & Sons, 1987.

Fisk, George. *Marketing Systems*. New York: Harper & Row, 1967.

Gist, Ronald R. *Marketing and Society*. New York: Rinehart & Winston, 1971.

Gross, Charles W. *Marketing Concepts and Decision Making*. St. Paul, MN: West Publishing Company, 1987.

Halbert, M. *The Meaning and Sources of Marketing Theory*. New York: McGraw-Hill Book Company, 1965.

Haughney, John D. *Effective Catalogs*. New York: John Wiley & Sons, 1968.

Heskett, James L. *Marketing*. New York: Macmillan Publishing Company, 1976.

Hill, Richard M., Ralph S. Alexander, and James S. Cross. *Industrial Marketing*, 4th ed. Homewood, IL: Richard D. Irwin, 1975.

Hodgson, Richard S. *The Dartnell Direct Mail and Mail Order Handbook*, 2nd ed. Chicago: Dartnell Corporation, 1974.

Holloway, Robert J., and Robert S. Hancock. *Marketing in a Changing Environment*, 2nd ed. New York: John Wiley & Sons, 1973.

Howard, J. A. *Marketing Management, Operating, Strategic and Administrative*. Homewood, IL: Richard D. Irwin, 1973.

Hunt, Shelby D. *Marketing Theory: the Philosophy of Marketing Science*. Homewood, IL: Richard D. Irwin, 1983.

Kelley, E. J. *Marketing Strategy and Functions*. Englewood Cliffs, NJ: Prentice-Hall, 1957.

Kolter, Philip. *Marketing Management, Analysis, Planning and Control*. Englewood Cliffs, NJ: Prentice-Hall, 1972.

Kolter, Philip. *Marketing Management*, 2nd ed. Englewood Cliffs, NJ: Prentice-Hall, 1972.

Lazer, William. *Marketing Management: A Systems Perspective*. New York: John Wiley & Sons, 1971.

Lipson, Harry A., and John R. Darling. *Introduction to Marketing*. New York: John Wiley & Sons, 1971.

Lynn, Robert A. *Price Policies and Marketing Management*. Homewood, IL: Richard D. Irwin, 1967.

McCarthy, J. E. *Basic Marketing*, 4th ed. Homewood, IL: Richard D. Irwin, 1960.

Martyn, Sean. *How to Start and Run a Successful Mail Order Business*. New York: McKay, 1971.

Matthews, John B., Jr., Robert D. Buzzell, Theodore Levitt, and Ronald E. Frank. *Marketing: An Introductory Analysis*. New York: McGraw-Hill Book Company, 1964.

Melcher, Daniel, and Nancy Larrick. *Printing and Promotion Handbook: How to Plan, Produce and Use Printing, Advertising and Direct Mail*, 3rd ed. New York: McGraw-Hill Book Company, 1966.

Phillips, Charles F. *Marketing by Manufacturers*, rev. ed. Chicago: Richard D. Irwin, 1951.

Phillips, Charles F., and Delbert J. Duncan. *Marketing Principles and Methods*, 6th ed. Homewood, IL: Richard D. Irwin, 1968.

Pride, William M., and O. C. Farrell. *Marketing: Basic Concepts and Decisions*. Boston: Houghton Mifflin Company, 1986.

Revzan, David A. *Wholesaling in Marketing Organization*. New York: John Wiley & Sons, 1961.

Rewoldt, Stewart H., James D. Scott, and Martin R. Warshaw. *Introduction to Marketing Management*. Homewood, IL: Richard D. Irwin, 1973.

Risley, George. *Modern Industrial Marketing: A Decision Making Approach*. New York: McGraw-Hill Book Company, 1972.

Rosenbloom, Bert. *Marketing Functions and the Wholesaler-Distributor: Achieving Excellence in Distribution*. Washington, DC: National Association of Wholesaler-Distributors, 1988.

Simon, Julian L. *How to Start and Operate a Mail Order Business*. New York: McGraw-Hill Book Company, 1965.

Smykay, Edward W. *Physical Distribution Management*, 3rd ed. New York: Macmillan Book Company, 1973.

Sparks, Howard. *The Amazing Mail Order Business and How to Succeed in It*. New York: Feld, 1966.

Stansfield, Richard H. *The Dartnell Advertising Managers' Handbook*, 2nd ed. Chicago: Dartnell Corporation, 1975.

Stanton, William J. *Fundamentals of Marketing*, 3rd ed. New York: McGraw-Hill Book Company, 1971.

Stern, Louis W., and Adel I. El-Ansary. *Marketing Channels*. Englewood Cliffs, NJ: Prentice-Hall Publishing Company, 1988.

Walters, C. Glenn. *Marketing Channels*. New York: Ronald Press Company, 1974.

Wish, John R., and Stephen H. Gambel. *Marketing and Social Issues*. New York: John Wiley & Sons, 1971.

Zikmund, William, and Michael D'Amico. *Marketing*. New York: John Wiley & Sons, 1984.

Index

About the Author

NICHOLAS T. SCHEEL is founder and editor of *Drop Shipping News*, a trade publication devoted to all facets of drop shipping, particularly in reference to mail order. Mr. Scheel has been a Vice President of Consolidated Marketing Services, Inc., a firm specializing in direct response advertising and marketing services.